Women, Jewish Law and Modernity

New Opportunities in a Post-Feminist Age

Women, Jewish Law and Modernity

New Opportunities in a Post-Feminist Age

by

Joel B. Wolowelsky

KTAV Publishing House, Inc.
1997

Library of Congress Cataloging-in-Publication Data

Wolowelsky, Joel B.
Women, Jewish law and modernity : new opportunities in a post-feminist age / by Joel B. Wolowelsky.
p. cm.
Includes bibliographical references.
ISBN 0-88125-574-2
1. Women in Judaism. 2. Orthodox Judaism—United States. 3. Judaism—20th century. I. Title.
BM729.W6W65 1997
296.8'32'082—dc21 96-29693
CIP

Manufactured in the United States of America
KTAV Publishing House, Inc.
900 Jefferson St., Hoboken, NJ 07030

For Rebecca, Naomi, and Aviya

Contents

Preface

Halakhically committed Jews living in a secular society often find their core principles under attack, both from within and without the Jewish community. We are obligated to fight for our religious principles regardless of whether or not they are popular; nevertheless, it is both pointless and counterproductive to replay yesterday's battles when the rules of engagement have changed. There is no halakhic imperative requiring us to automatically reject proposals simply because they are innovative when they no longer pose a threat to Torah values.

To take an example from not so long ago, opponents of the nascent Reform movement fought strongly against sermons in the vernacular, for in their view such innovations emanated from assimilationist principles. Whether or not this strategy was appropriate when adopted, surely no one today would take up the cry against sermons in English. Indeed, they are now part of the arsenal of Torah.

There is no doubt that feminism as a movement has

included themes antithetical to halakhic values, such as abortion on demand, support for lesbianism, dedication to a unisex society lacking gender-specific roles, and so on. Given the overall friction between feminist ideology and halakhah, Orthodox leaders have been suspicious of arguably constructive suggestions for increased women's participation in religious activities on the grounds that accepting them could legitimize feminism in the eyes of the halakhic community.

It is now time to move past this fear of feminism. We are fast approaching a post-feminist age in which accepting specific proposals originally promoted by feminists no longer carries the implication that we accept feminist ideology as a whole. For example, providing full access to education and professions based on merit and not gender, eliminating sexual exploitation, and maintaining equal pay for men and women doing substantially the same jobs are no longer associated with the objectionable aspects of the feminist movement. Thus, today, support for equal access to jobs is not automatically linked to support for unhampered access to abortions. Women now combine loyalty to traditional values like childrearing with modern professional goals; women who fought for the right to enter the highest echelons of their professions now feel little guilt when they take off time to raise a family.

However, halakhically committed women do insist that, with very few exceptions, dissimilar opportunities for advancement should not be based on gender differences. A woman might forgo the opportunity to enter the fast track leading to a law firm partnership, for example, because she chooses to spend more time at home raising her family. She would not, however, be willing to accept the proposition that women should not be allowed to compete for such jobs because they cannot understand the intricacies of tax law. This is a position with which the halakhic community should be quite comfortable.

It is time to carry over this attitude to a broader range of activities designed to increase women's involvement in religious ritual and practice. Originally, some of the members of the Modern Orthodox community who pushed for greater participation by women in religious activities might have been motivated in part by feminist ideology. Now, however, due to the unparalleled growth in Torah education, advocacy of women's participation is clearly driven by a desire for religious growth. As we shall later point out, Rabbi Moshe Feinstein's position on such increased involvement is that the motivation of the women determines the halakhic reaction.

The motivation surrounding women's desire for change has shifted over the years. Consequently, in appropriate circumstances there should be a corresponding change in our religious community's response. We should not continue to fight yesterday's battles, confusing a genuine desire to grow in Torah with an attack on Torah values. It is obvious to those who have first-hand contact with women engaged in advanced Torah education in Israeli schools like Michlelet Lindenbaum ("Brovender's"), Matan, or Nishmat, or in American schools like Drisha and Stern College, that it is the unparalleled high levels of education attained by these women that now drives their desire for comparable growth in religious life, not any particular feminist agenda.

Thus we take for granted that when halakhah allows for it, and the motivations are religious in nature, we should encourage increased involvement for women in all areas of Jewish life—in our homes, at our life-cycle celebrations, in our synagogues, and in our yeshivot—to enable women to enrich their spiritual lives. We should not be embarrassed about our position, nor should we allow ourselves to be dismissed or marginalized as proponents of either anti-halakhic feminism or the equally antinomian egalitarianism taking hold in the Conservative movement. The possibilities should be explored in classical halakhic terms, with reference to classic texts and recognized authorities—not as skirmishes in a battle against the feminist bogey-person. As we shall see, these discussions are part and parcel of legitimate halakhic discourse.

We should not hesitate to shift our reaction from suspicion to encouragement. Decades ago, serious formal Torah education for women was proposed only as a *be-di'avad,* a stopgap innovation to counter the negative situation created by women pursuing advanced secular education. Now it is a *lekhateḥilah* desideratum. Educators across the spectrum of Orthodoxy now take pride in advanced women's seminaries. We hear few cries to go back to "the good old days" when women were unlettered and often illiterate. It is time for a *lekhateḥilah* encouragement of increased women's involvement in a wide spectrum of religious activities.

In doing so, we must be willing to question the motivation behind all proposed innovations. Thus, for example, when we discuss women's prayer groups, we do not hesitate to oppose those protocols which have the appearance of mimicry despite the fact that they may pass technical muster. Similarly, we propose tempering women's public involvement in wedding ceremonies with appreciation of other public policy concerns. Such hesitations, however, should not paralyze us from moving ahead when we can and should.

The explorations in this book grew out of real deliberations with students and friends who consider women's increased involvement in religious life most natural, but who would not act on their intuitions until they had explored their halakhic integrity. Unfortunately, all too many of the authorities they consulted either could not put aside their fear of feminism or, afraid of condemnation by their colleagues, would not publicly voice their private sympathies.

Not everything suggested here is appropriate for all people in all communities. What everyone should welcome, however, is both the opportunity to explore the possibilities in a halakhic context and the freedom to suggest additional areas to explore. Over the next decades, some of the suggestions made here will no doubt become as natural as advanced Torah study for women is today; others will not be as appealing; still others, as yet unexplored, will emerge as pressing concerns. That is how it should be.

In discussing these topics over the past years, I have been fortunate in having a large circle of friends who were generous in challenging perspectives, raising my consciousness, suggesting and learning through halakhic sources, and debating preliminary presentations. They are primarily my colleagues at the Yeshivah of Flatbush; friends whom I met while a faculty member at the Mount Scopus College Counterpoint Seminars, the Flatbush-Ramaz Freshman Seminars, and the Yeshiva University Inter-yeshiva Seminars; fellow members of the Editorial Board of *Tradition* and the Steering Committee of the Orthodox Forum; and inquisitive and searching students, including some who grew up to become close friends. There is no way to mention them all, although I feel obligated to single out two: my colleague and teacher, Rabbi Pinchos Zelig Prag, who graciously and generously shares his encyclopedic knowledge of Torah sources, never allowing his personal viewpoint to cloud his willingness to explore all perspectives with sensitivity and integrity; and my ofttimes *ḥavruta,* Joseph J. Feit, whose long friendship and wise counsel I greatly value. I am also thankful to Bernard Scharfstein and his most competent staff at KTAV Publishing House for much-appreciated advice and encouragement. Needless to say, I alone bear responsibility for this presentation.

Many of the discussions here appeared in more preliminary presentations in *Judaism, Modern Judaism, Teḥumin,* and *Tradition.* I am indebted to the respective editors of these distinguished journals for the opportunity to have been able to explore these topics with their readers. Those essays and the subsequent discussions they stimulated form the core of the book.

I am grateful for the opportunity to lovingly dedicate this discussion to Rebecca, Naomi, and Aviya Krieger, who grew and grow in an atmosphere where commitment to Torah and full participation in religious, communal, and intellectual activities is taken for granted; and to thank their parents, David and Marsha, for too many things to list here, but which are best encapsulated in the warm way they make me feel that I am truly at home when I join them for my extended visits in Jerusalem.

Joel B. Wolowelsky
Yom Yerushalayim 5756

Introduction

Hannah's Voice

The biblical story of Hannah in the opening chapter of the book of Samuel is well known. She was barren and suffering for it. Each year she would accompany her husband, Elkanah, and his fertile second wife, Peninnah, to worship and offer sacrifice at Shiloh. Each year she would be tormented to tears by Peninnah's taunts to the point where she could not eat. Frustrated by his inability to correct the situation, her husband, Elkanah, said to her, "Hannah, why are you crying, and why aren't you eating? Why are you so sad? Am I not more devoted to you than ten sons?"

Unconsoled, Hannah went to the sanctuary to pour out her heart to God. Eli the priest watched her, noticing that her lips were moving without making a sound. Regular worshipers, he knew, spoke their prayers aloud, so he took her for a drunk. Eli said to her, "How long will you make a drunken spectacle of yourself? Sober up!" And Hannah replied, "Oh, no, my lord! I am a very unhappy woman. I have drunk no wine or other strong drink, but I have been pouring out my heart to the Lord." "Then go in peace," said Eli, "and may the God of Israel grant what you have asked of Him."

At first glance, Elkanah's consoling remarks are nothing but touching. He is fertile, as evidenced by Peninnah's children. He empathizes with Hannah's unfulfilled life, but can do nothing to help other than offer his devoted love and commitment.

Malbim, however, reads Elkanah's statement with a slightly different tone. Elkanah is somewhat bewildered at Hannah's depression. There are only two reasons, he argues, for wanting children. One either wants to fulfill God's command to reproduce or fears facing old age without the support of children. Hannah (like all women) is not obligated by the mitzvah of reproduction, for it pertains only to men. And as for the protection offered by one's offspring, Elkanah can provide the support of ten children. "Why are you crying, and why aren't you eating?" he asks her. "Why are you so sad?"

His response, continues Malbim, drove Hannah to the sanctuary. She had never doubted the efficacy of prayer; but until then she had relied on Elkanah's prayers on her behalf. Once she realized that he did not feel her pain and hence could not advocate before God on her behalf, she went herself to pray in God's presence.

Eli, too, could not appreciate Hannah's predicament. Focusing on form, he noted that she had taken a nontraditional approach to prayer: speaking from the heart, not by way of her vocal chords. Having no other way to interpret her action, he condemned her at first. But later, when he became aware of her sincerity, he blessed her. "Then go in peace," said Eli, "and may the God of

Israel grant what you have asked of Him." And, indeed, the Talmud uses Hannah's prayer as the paradigm of true and authentic prayer.

This story forms an appropriate foreshadowing of the contemporary situation in the traditional Jewish community. Motivated by their unprecedented high level of Jewish education, women have been expanding their participation in areas of traditional religious life from which they heretofore have been excluded or exempted. Many religious leaders cannot understand why women seek these innovations. Some respond in sympathy with Elkanah. There is no halakhic obligation for women to take on these additional roles, they argue; what positive agenda could motivate such demands? Have we not provided a positive religious community for men and women alike?

Others respond in sympathy with Eli. There is only one explanation for such deviations from tradition, they say. Only the heresies of religious reform and contemporary feminism could inspire such demands. These women must be drunk from the spirits of feminism; they should be admonished and rejected.

Indeed, modern halakhically committed Jews may find themselves more closely aligned with Eli than Elkanah. Insensitivity to another's pain is intolerable. But that does not justify each and every personal response to such pain. As much as one might wish to meet the needs of another, halakhah provides a matrix within which one must work. When, for example, Susan Grossman, a non-Orthodox rabbi, writes that "Judaism and feminism are two ethical systems which command my allegiance and guide my actions,"[1] she articulates what is most objectionable to the halakhically committed.

Different ideologies may sometimes create a creative tension or even compete for one's attention. But for the halakhically committed Jew, it is only Torah that can command true loyalty. Yet, as Eli found, not everything that seems out of step with traditional form is out of step with halakhah. In fact, some new forms may well be the harbingers of enriching and religiously significant traditions.

Seeing past Elkanah's insensitivity and avoiding falling into Eli's trap is no small feat. Differentiating between a voice expressed in the context of Torah and mitzvah, on the one hand, and one couched within a framework of halakhic indifference, on the other, takes time, calmness, and self-confidence. Traditionally, men are forbidden to hear *kol ishah,* a woman's voice. (Of course, the prohibition applies to potentially sexually evocative situations, not the sound of a woman's voice in, say, everyday conversation.) Yet, former Chief Rabbi Ovadiah Yosef remarked in a different context that in an atmosphere of Torah and mitzvah, there is no need to fear the prohibition of *kol ishah.*[2]

A Torah Response

Learning to respond appropriately to the voice we hear requires thought and perspective. One must avoid hearing a challenge in every query. More often than not, the women seeking increased religious opportunities are simply exploring the implications of their committed Torah lifestyle in the modern world.

To be sure, one must respond honestly. Unless one is committed to an educational policy deliberately designed to keep people ignorant, one cannot claim that all the authorities forbid something when a literate questioner will soon discover that this is false. Lying may be effective in the short run, but eventually it is destructive to the integrity that should be the hallmark of our religious life. Clearly, honesty also requires avoiding simplistic answers to complex questions. For example, *tzeniut* (modesty) is a core value in the halakhic community. But one cannot simply dismiss a suggestion by invoking the cry of modesty when our community regularly accepts analogous activities as modest and acceptable. Also, it should not ipso facto disturb us that others within the Torah community do not accept everything that we do. For example, many married women in the "yeshiva world" cover their hair with a wig, not feeling undermined by the cries of impropriety leveled against them by certain Torah scholars who feel that women's hair should be covered with a cloth. Unanimity has never been the sine qua non of halakhic legitimacy.

Torah leaders responding to questions must have confidence that the questioner respects halakhic authority. Religious Jews understand that the personal interaction between questioner and respondent is at the heart of the halakhic system. Healthy congregants understand that it may be unwise to actualize certain things that are technically permitted. There is no need to see every individual question as but a detail in a broader antinomian campaign, thereby requiring the creation of arbitrary "fences to the law."

It is true that many religious women are not troubled by their status within the traditional community. Nonetheless, there is a need to anticipate questions and provide answers—even tentative ones—before they are asked. There will be movement on these issues even if we pretend to be deaf to the current discussion; it is an outgrowth of the world in which we live. Leading instead of reacting helps to ensure that things will evolve in conformity to basic halakhic values. Waiting, in the hope that situations will not surface, almost guarantees an eventual confrontation.

Two responsa by *gedolei Torah* provide a model for dealing with the questions that arise in this area. The first is a classic responsum of the late Rabbi Yeḥiel Yaakov Weinberg,[3] whose standing as a major halakhic authority of the postwar generation is universally recognized. It deals with a question put to him by the officers of the Yeshurun Society, an organization of religious college-age French youths.

R. Weinberg was asked whether young men and women might sit at the same table and sing zemirot together at the organization's Friday night Ongei Shabbat. His *teshuvah* contains solid halakhic analysis; but what concerns us here are his introductory and closing comments. The issue, he concedes, is not clear-cut. Nonetheless, the Orthodox rabbinic leaders of Germany had allowed and sometimes even encouraged coed activity of this kind because, he posits, they were experts in the discipline of education and had succeeded in raising entire generations of young people who feared God and were well educated secularly. "Now," he writes, "rabbis from Poland and Hungary who have found their way to France strongly oppose these new approaches that the French Orthodox rabbis instituted based on the system of Germany's gaonim."

As committed as he was to the letter and spirit of the law, R. Weinberg had no fear regarding the halakhic difficulties involved in allowing coed singing to continue. His model was R. Yisrael Salanter, who had reported that when visiting Germany he had seen R. Esriel Hildesheimer conducting a shiur in Tanakh and Shulḥan Arukh for young women. R. Salanter's reaction, recorded in the Seridei Esh, is pointed: "If a rabbi in Lita [Lithuania] tried to introduce such an activity in his community, he would certainly be removed from his position. And indeed, this is the law. Nonetheless, I hope that I can share R. Hildesheimer's place in Gan Eden. The reason is: *et la'asot,* this is a time to act."

Thus, argues R. Weinberg, Yeshurun should continue to follow the policies of *gedolei Ashkenaz,* the halakhic authorities of German Jewry. "They understood the mindset of the young women of that generation, who were well educated and knew languages and science. These young women had strong feelings of self-respect and took offense and rejection when excluded from participating in the zemirot."[4] This, he concludes, is obvious to anyone who knows the nature of the women in these countries. To be deaf to their request to participate in the zemirot would be to drive them from the Torah community.[5]

The second responsum is that of Rabbi Moshe Feinstein, halakhic master of our own generation. It takes up the question of whether a woman may wear a tallit during tefillah. After explaining his understanding of the reason for exempting women from the mitzvah of tzitzit, R. Feinstein spoke harshly against those who were proposing this change from the tradition of women not wearing a tallit. "No battle will help, for there is no power to effect a change—even with the consent of the whole world. And those stubborn women who want to fight for change are to be regarded as deniers of the Torah."[6] In the end, though, he concedes that a woman *may* wear a tallit if her impetus is to perform the mitzvah; he does not like the motivation of the specific woman in question, but acknowledges that in general halakhah does not prohibit women from wearing a tallit.

> Every woman has the right to perform those mitzvot in which the Torah has not obligated her. . . . Our custom is that they perform the mitzvot of shofar and lulav and recite the blessings over them. This is applicable to tzitzit. Therefore, a woman who wants to wear a garment that differs in style from that of men but has four corners that obligate it in tzitzit may observe this mitzvah.

R. Weinberg establishes the principle that the societal context of the women involved is a legitimate factor to be considered in establishing a Torah approach to a situation. R. Feinstein establishes the principle that one must be attentive to the attitudes informing a request for broadened participation in religious life. The objective permissibility of wearing the tallit must be acknowledged, but it is not the only determining factor. One must resist any attempt to import foreign ideologies, such as gender egalitarianism, into the Torah community, even if the forms used cannot be objected to on technical grounds. But when women make these requests out of a desire for genuine religious growth, they should be allowed the maximum opportunity to progress to their full religious potential.

It would be safe to say that most members of the modern traditional camp appreciate the mindset of the women members of Yeshurun and empathize with R. Weinberg's understanding of the situation. We sense that the members of Yeshurun were not engaging in any social protest. We understand that they wanted to join the zemirot only because they saw it as a simple extension of their everyday modest lifestyle, a position with which we are quite comfortable. Having been admitted to a coed university to study science and language, they did not wish to be excluded from a Tanakh class or the zemirot singing.

On the other hand, the image of a woman in shul wearing a tallit probably evokes little sympathy even in the Modern Orthodox community. Women are exempt from the mitzvah of lulav as well as tzitzit. Yet, while we take for granted a woman exercising her option to perform the mitzvah of lulav, somehow we assume that the woman wearing a tallit in shul is making some sort of demonstration in the women's section. We conclude that she is wearing the man's traditional black-striped tallit to make a point, perhaps to attack the basic halakhic premise that men and women sometimes have distinctive roles to play in the Jewish community.

But, like Eli, we may be misleading ourselves into focusing on familiarity of form over integrity of content. Most of us have little association with specially designed women's tallitot, which, as R. Feinstein suggested, are made to conform to the halakhic requirements for tzitzit but look like modest female garb. Far from evoking any sense of protest, these creative tallitot enable a woman to perform an optional mitzvah, encourage *tzeniut* in dress, and work against the style-consciousness prevalent in many synagogues. As R. Feinstein notes, there is no reason to oppose these tallitot if they are worn to fulfill an optional mitzvah.

Echoes do not constitute an authentic voice. When we hear a new proposal, we must make sure of what we are hearing. As new suggestions are made, we must be sure that we have first-hand knowledge of what is being proposed. Otherwise one might join Eli in opposing something that is not there.

We also need not shy away from admitting that our discussions assume a changed perspective on the position of women within our religious community. We can take our cue from the changed attitude toward women expressed at the Passover Seder.

"On all other nights we eat upright or reclining," reads the Haggadah, "but on this night we *all* recline [as a sign of our free status]." Yet despite the general obligation of women to participate in the Seder, the original talmudic ruling was that "a woman who is in the presence of her husband does not recline, but if she is an important woman, she must recline."[7]

Rashbam explains that she may not recline because "the fear of her husband is upon her, as she is subjugated to him."[8] Commenting on this, R. Ḥayyim David Halevi, Chief Rabbi of Tel Aviv, rules that:

> the rationale for this ruling has expired, and therefore the halakhah should be changed. Perhaps in different times or places the fear of a woman's husband was upon her and she was subjugated to him. However, this is not true nowadays, as no woman is subjugated to her husband and the fear of him is not upon her. She therefore must recline.[9]

Kesef Mishneh quotes Sefer Manoah's criteria for "an important woman": (1) she has no husband whom she must serve and is the head of her household; (2) she is creative and productive (*befri yadeha*); (3) she is the daughter of the generation's leading scholar; (4) she has maids and servants who relieve her from the duties of preparing the Passover meal (which would otherwise take precedence over her duty to recline at the meal).[10]

What catches our attention here is not the problem

of why a woman might be exempted if even a poor man or a male servant is required to recline. It is the ruling of the Mordekhai,[11] endorsed and codified by Rema,[12] that "all of our women are important and must recline."

What did this ruling mean? It could not have meant that *all* women fit into one of these four categories. It would not take a learned essay to prove that no such society ever existed. Clearly we are talking about the perceptions of women in the times of the Mordekhai and Rema. The undistinguished wife in a poor family, burdened with household responsibilities, is "important." Whether or not she herself or her husband perceives her as such, she must recline. A ruling that "all our women are important and must recline" cannot be read as describing the individual reality in each and every household. Rather, it prescribes a general *Anschauung* with respect to the status of women at that time. Once it was established that "all our women are important," an individual wife and her husband lost the option of her not reclining in order to serve the meal. "She must recline." Similarly, when we look around the halakhic community and realize that "all our women are educated and literate," we shall come to unavoidable conclusions about their participation in various traditional activities.

Some Ashkenazic commentators maintain that, inasmuch as it is not the current custom in general society for prominent women to recline while eating, women at the Seder may still not be obligated to do so, as the goal was only to mimic the behavior of the rich at their regular meals.[13] But no one holds the opinion that the principle is no longer operative or that those women who do not meet the suggested technical criteria for "importance" should adopt the talmudic position that they are not important. All women in our religious community are important, just as they are all educated and literate. This is a reality that we must confront with honesty, integrity, and courage.

Modern Orthodoxy

It would be fair to say that the locus of the present discussion is primarily the Modern Orthodox community. Like all members of the halakhic community, Modern Orthodox Jews define their lives in terms of halakhic values and commitments. They have the same allegiance to Torah and its teachers as those to the "right," but nonetheless maintain a distinct image. Their rabbis tend to have studied at Yeshiva University's Rabbi Isaac Elchanan Theological Seminary and/or belong to the Rabbinical Council of America. Modern Orthodox Jews are inclined to pray at a Young Israel or another shul affiliated with the Union of Orthodox Jewish Congregations of America. All *gedolei Torah* are revered, but the community's halakhic and intellectual master has been the Rav, the late Rabbi Joseph B. Soloveitchik.

Certainly openness to secular studies is not limited to Modern Orthodoxy. Yeshiva University has no monopoly on doctors and lawyers who are talmidei ḥakhamim, although it can claim a much higher percentage than, say, the Lakewood Yeshiva. However, openness to the liberal arts (as opposed to the professions) and to Western traditions is something that distinguishes Modern Orthodoxy from the "right." (One could not imagine, for example, a gadol ha-dor other than the Rav setting out to examine "the pervasive state of mind of Western man who has become estranged from himself, a state with which *all of us as Westerners* [emphasis added] are acquainted."[13]) Thus, the fact that some attitude or problem may grow out of the modern experience does not make it ipso facto illegitimate. For those more insulated from the Western experience, the alien nature of an issue makes it automatically suspect. But those who function in the day-to-day Western world will tend to reject that with which they are familiar only when it contradicts halakhic norms.

Religious Zionism certainly prevails in the Modern Orthodox community. Its members strongly identify both with the Hesder yeshiva students who fulfill their responsibility to Torah and the State of Israel by combining army service with advanced Torah study and with those who belong to the Kibbutz ha-Dati movement. So strong is this identification that it often comes as a surprise to Modern Orthodox Americans that the "modern" religious society in Israel does not share their concern regarding women's issues, itself arguably one of the practical defining characteristics of Modern Orthodoxy.

But it really should not be surprising at all. Religious society mirrors its more general setting. Israeli attitudes are shaped both by the Middle Eastern experience (in which women have a distinct place in the general culture) and by defense needs (which assign very different roles to men and women as they enter their adult years). American society grants far more equal access to men and women in all areas of life. Many Israeli rabbis have little secular education and, unlike many American Orthodox rabbis from across the spectrum, have insufficient shared vocabulary with Western-oriented Israelis (whether or not the latter are committed to *shemirat Shabbat*).

Israeli community rabbis report to the state's rabbinic establishment and not their balebatim. They have little reason to be involved in discussions about issues that do not concern them. Questions are posed only when people think that answers might be forthcoming.

No doubt many issues that we shall discuss here grow out of our specifically American milieu. But to say this is not to cast aspersions on the halakhic validity of these questions. All halakhic questions grow out of the daily experience of committed Jews, whatever the area of life under consideration. But while the questions legitimately grow out of the general societal experience, the answers must emerge from our specific halakhic commitments.

Modern Orthodox women function day to day in a world that respects their manifold abilities. They naturally assume that they will not be excluded from the privileges of power, be the setting a college or high school faculty, a board of directors, a community board, or a professional association. They expect to join the school or shul board of trustees and resent being assigned to a sisterhood or ladies auxiliary. If some women are principals, other women will assume that they have legitimate contributions to make to the board of education. A shul member who has earned an M.B.A. degree will quite naturally feel that it is appropriate for her to be on the budget committee. Those who have achieved a high level of Torah learning will take for granted that it is appropriate for them to be on the religion and education committees of their synagogues.

We need make no apologies for welcoming this reality. Some authorities argue that the Torah's injunction to "set over yourselves a king" (Deuteronomy 17:15), which is interpreted to mean "a king but not a queen," precludes a woman's assuming such communal roles. However, Rabbi J. David Bleich outlines the counter-argument:

> Nowhere is there an indication that women are to be excluded from purely honorific positions. Under contemporary conditions, synagogue officials and boards of directors have no power of coercion at all. They rely on the good will of synagogue members for compliance. . . . Under such circumstances the officers of a congregation do not exercise even an approximation of royal power, since they cannot in any way compel compliance. If women are excluded only from communal positions of authority in which the officeholder is endowed with coercive authority, it may be argued that, under present conditions, women are not precluded from holding synagogue office.[14]

Parents whose children attend a Modern Orthodox yeshiva may have no interest in their daughters serving as *ba'alot keriah* in shul. Yet they would certainly object to their daughters being automatically excluded from advanced math or biology classes. Indeed, it becomes more and more natural for us to question all acts of exclusion. We find ourselves asking whether various policies are really mandated by halakhah and reflective of its ethical system.

Opportunity vs. Obligation

There are, however, some points that will irreconcilably divide us from others who press for greater women's participation in traditional Jewish activities. We are committed to the basic halakhic structure of distinctiveness of obligation. Unlike other Jewish groups that have, for example, discarded the priestly status of Kohanim, we feel no moral outrage that only a Kohen may ascend the synagogue *dukhan* to invoke God's blessing on the congregation. Regarding those mitzvot observed by both men and women, we take for granted that *gadol ha-metzuveh ve-oseh mi-mi she-eino metzuveh ve-oseh*—it is religiously more significant to perform a mitzvah out of a sense of obligation than as an allowable option.[15] This may go against the contemporary sensibility that regards religious volunteerism as an ideal and egalitarianism as a fundamental religious value; but it is a cornerstone of halakhic reasoning.

Generally speaking, women are exempted from those mitzvot that require that something be done within a specific time frame (*mitzvot assei she-ha-zeman gramma*). Rabbi Emanuel Rackman suggests that "in order that man learn to sanctify time, the Law ordains for him many commandments which are governed by a calendar and a clock. Women, on the other hand, by the very nature of their physical constitution and the requirements of the Law regarding their menstrual periods, needed little more to make them aware of the sanctity of time."[16]

However, Rabbi Saul Berman points out that an examination of the sources shows that the principle of exempting women from time-bound affirmative mitzvot is less than exact. In fact, women are obligated to perform many of these mitzvot (such as reciting Kiddush on Shabbat and eating matzah on Passover). Indeed, women are obligated to perform as many time-bound mitzvot as the number from which they are exempted.

Noting that the common denominator of those mitzvot from which women are exempt is a communal appearance involved in performing them, R. Berman concludes:

> The underlying motive of exemption would then be neither the attempt to unjustly deprive women of the opportunity to achieve religious fulfillment, nor the proposition that women are inherently more religiously sensitive. Rather, exemption would be a tool used by the Torah to achieve a particular social goal, namely to assure that no legal obligation would interfere with the selection by Jewish women of a role that was centered almost exclusively in the home. However, it is vital to emphasize that even with these exemptions, the wife-mother-homemaker role is not the mandated, or exclusively proper role, though it is clearly the preferred and therefore protected role.[17]

Whether or not we agree with this analysis, we must recognize the halakhic reality that just as we do not have the option of declaring that any mitzvah is not binding and obligatory, we cannot impose an obligation that does not exist. But lack of obligation does not mean lack of opportunity. One need not look past the mitzvah of shofar, for example, to see that while women are not required to hear the blowing of the shofar, synagogue officials go out of their way to announce the schedule so that women not be denied the opportunity to participate in what for them is an optional mitzvah.[18]

R. Weinberg had noted, regarding those who opposed granting women the right to vote, that "one can rebut and debate the sources [*le-palpel*], but there is no point to it, as there are deeper issues involved."[20] Time, not logical debate, will eventually settle the controversy, he concluded. So too with many of the issues under discussion here. Nevertheless, the discussion involved in responding to the contemporary *kol ishah* must include a detailed discussion of the technical halakhic considerations. It is this analysis, coupled with the motivation of the questioner, which lends authenticity to the discussion.

Rabbinic authorities have an obligation to protect the integrity of halakhah, and not simply to decide technical issues of "permitted or forbidden." There is no denying that this responsibility should color our approach to contemporary women's issues. Currently, egalitarianism encourages women to participate in certain areas of tradition even when doing so cannot be justified by a halakhic argument. To allow women to participate in areas that until now they have avoided (whether or not technically permitted to them), it might be argued, would be to confuse those unlettered in halakhic sources and encourage a non-halakhic, egalitarian approach.

On the other hand, one might maintain that when authorities forbid what is actually permitted, they strengthen the hands of those who say that rabbinic prohibitions in this area flow from personal biases rather than halakhic commitment, and in the end encourage the proponents of egalitarianism. This is a most legitimate debate. Unfortunately, notes Esther Krauss, director of the Shalhevet Torah Institute for Women,

> any issue related to women evokes irrational fears in all segments of the Orthodox community. It often distorts judgment, causes otherwise fair and rational people to draw unconfirmed conclusions, and usually brings out the least kind and generous qualities of normally sensitive and respectful people. All this is to the detriment of the Jewish community, for it prevents us and our leaders from dealing with a major issue confronting Orthodox Judaism today.[21]

Two Eves in Eden

Rabbi Soloveitchik's analysis of the two Adams of the first two chapters of the Bible has provided an approach for appreciating the role of the man of faith in contemporary society. An analogous analysis of the "two Eves" should provide us with an approach to the tension felt by contemporary observant women concerned with broadening their participation in the halakhic community.

The Rav noted that the differences between the two biblical creation stories reflect a real contradiction in the nature of man. The Adam of the first chapter, commanded to "fill the earth and subdue it," searches for dignity in the world.

> In doing all this, Adam the first is trying to carry out the mandate entrusted to him by his Maker. . . . It is God who decreed that the story of Adam the first be the great saga of freedom of man-slave who gradually transforms himself into man-master. While pursuing this goal, driven by an urge which he cannot but obey, Adam the first transcends the limits of the reasonable and probable and ventures into the open spaces of a boundless universe. . . . Man reaching for the distant stars is acting in harmony with his nature which was created, willed, and directed by his maker.[22]

Adam the second, however, seeks to submit himself to God, to merge into the *masorah* (tradition) community, which transcends the centuries of its individual members.

But these are but pure typologies. There is no true Adam the first or Adam the second. We all have both Adams within ourselves and move back and forth between these two poles of the human personality.

> Man is a dialectical being; an inner schism runs through his personality at every level. . . . The Judaic view posits that the schism is willed by God as the source of man's greatness and his election as a singular charismatic being. Man is great and creative because he is torn by conflict and is always in a state of ontological tenseness and perplexity.[23]

To try to live as only one or the other of the two Adams is to lose half of one's human identity—and to forfeit the creativity that accompanies the struggle to actualize and not compromise both aspects of one's existence.

Extending this analysis, we should expect to find two Eves paralleling the two Adams. Eve the first was created as a full partner with Adam the first—"male and female He created them"—and shares his legitimate urge to control nature, to know and understand. And Eve the second also searches for membership in her *masorah* community.

> [People] are mistaken in thinking that there is only one *Massora* and one *Massora* community: the community of the fathers. It is not true. We have two *massorot,* two traditions, two communities, two *shalshalot ha-kabbala*—the massora community of the fathers and that of the mothers.[24]

The male *masorah* is that of discipline of thought as well as discipline of action. The female *masorah* is the appreciation of the presence of the Almighty. "The fathers taught generations how to observe the Shabbat; mothers taught generations how to greet the Shabbat and how to enjoy her twenty-four-hour presence."[25]

Of course, these too are pure types; everyone is expected to both know the laws of Shabbat and appreciate its presence. The "dialectical halakhah" demands that here too people move back and forth between two approaches to the world.

Those for whom egalitarianism is the sole motivating force in their lives are focused only on the Eve-the-first existence. Those who reject in toto the demands of contemporary women do not appreciate the necessity of everyone living with the tension of two types of *masorah* communities. They all forfeit the creativity that comes with full allegiance to our dialectical existence.

On Citations and Hesitations

All this having been said, we now embark on a consideration of expanding the role of women in four main areas of religious life: the home, life-cycle celebrations, synagogue prayer, and Jewish education. The argument draws on classical halakhic sources and without embarrassment asserts a particular point of view, arguing that halakhah can and should legitimately accommodate religious women's desire for greater participation in Jewish religious life.

Citations are sometimes tedious but they are crucial. The religious integrity of any position taken must be justified by appealing not to rhetoric but to classical sources and authorities. This, however, is not to say that different or even opposing positions cannot emerge from a study of the sources. Halakhah is multidimensional, although our current religious climate tends to paint it as monolithic. One need not argue the exclusivity of any position, only its legitimacy.

Of course, one must be prepared to walk away from those positions that cannot be justified halakhically, no matter how appealing they might be on the surface. Yet the converse is also true. When a position can be grounded in classical halakhic arguments, we should not tolerate simply dismissing it because it is personally unappealing. Refusing to recognize the legitimacy of such arguments is no less a violation of the integrity of halakhah than is the substitution of rhetoric for sources.

However, hesitation is also required. Just as not everything kosher is healthy to eat, not everything permitted is religiously enhancing. But these decisions have to be framed for what they are—public-policy or personal-preference questions rather than halakhic issues. Once the halakhic legitimacy of an option is accepted, the debate on how far to go becomes tied to the specific time and place in which the discussion takes place. Different readers at different times will reach different conclusions.

Where to draw the line, when to move forward, and when to retreat despite halakhic arguments that can be developed to the contrary are, in the end, judgment calls—not halakhic rulings—that must be made on both an individual and a communal level.

In Our Homes

Family Minhag

Rather than beginning with a general discussion of public policy, it might be more productive to first focus on the evolving changes that are taking place in contemporary religious Jewish homes. When private strategies are worked out away from the rancor of public debate, calmer positions emerge.

Throughout the spectrum of the traditional community, the wife is perceived as the akeret ha-bayit, the person who has primary responsibility for overseeing day-to-day matters regarding child-raising, meals, and so forth. Yet for men and women in the modern religious community, strict sex-role differentiation need not apply across the board. True, halakhah is nonegalitarian; men and women have different levels of obligation and participation in various matters. But changing diapers, cooking, and doing sundry chores are not necessarily seen as exclusively women's work; respect for one's spouse mandates that they be shared whenever possible. (And, mutatis mutandis, learning Torah is not exclusively men's work.) Women may stay home—if they can afford it—to raise a family; however, we not only recognize but take for granted the legitimacy of a woman's complementing her family life with pursuing a career—be it in Torah education, law, social work, medicine, or business—for personal fulfillment and not simply financial relief.

Exactly how a modern religious couple divides its collective household duties is, quite naturally, a matter of private concern. In most spheres of family we take it for granted that mutual discussion, rather than unilateral dictates, should characterize the reconciliation of differing approaches and conventions. Yet somehow there is a sense that in matters of religious custom (minhag) the same flexibility is antithetical to halakhic values. In the minds of some, a wife is expected to leave her family customs at the ḥuppah and adopt the minhagim of her husband. Continuing her own customs is in some ways viewed as an attack on the tradition itself.

Such an approach misinterprets not only the wife's motivation but also the position of the tradition. Although there is only one Torah, Jewish communities around the world have developed unique minhagim of their own. Generally speaking, it is true that people are required to observe the custom of the place of their residence (assuming that it has one dominant custom) and children must follow the customs of their families. But there is more leeway than one might imagine in deciding what exactly is the minhag of the family.

In past ages, when communities were usually stable and relatively isolated, it was easy to define community minhagim. But in our mobile society, where people from different communities find themselves thrown together in new congregations, it is hard to formulate strict definitions. Nowadays, writes Rabbi Ḥayyim David Halevi, Chief Rabbi of Tel Aviv, we are dealing with a relatively new situation in which inhabitants of the same city maintain different halakhic traditions. Moving to a new community does not necessarily mean adopting new customs.[26] Indeed, anyone who has visited a new community sees strategies for handling such situations evolving. Sometimes the emerging congregation empowers its ḥazzan to decide whether *nusaḥ Ashkenaz* or *nusaḥ Sefard* is used for, say, *Kedushah*; sometimes one *nusaḥ* emerges as dominant, but the community adopts some customs of the other. Often a local minhag develops which becomes characteristic of the community. And although individuals who move to a new city are theoretically required to adopt all the customs of their new place of residence, many (if not most) keep their own *nusaḥ* in their private tefillah and conform to the congregation only in public matters.

Posekim (halakhic decisors) have likened what happens when a woman marries to the situation when a person moves from one community to another. An individual who moves to a new city embraces its customs, and it was expected that a wife, similarly, would adopt the minhagim of her husband. Indeed, as a practical matter, marriage often meant that the bride left her father's home and town for her husband's. These assumptions are no longer entirely valid.

Today, religiously "intermarried" couples often work out arrangements similar to the congregational agreements mentioned above, and such compromises should not be seen as compromising halakhah. As R. Halevi points out, the rule that family minhag follows that of the husband is simply a practical judicial way of ensuring *shalom bayit* (a peaceful home), not an absolute principle. "With regard to anything that does not affect *shalom bayit,* the wife can continue to follow her own family's customs."[27] In particular, he notes, "matters of prayer and worship of God, which go to the heart of the person, do not belong to the category of things that can upset *shalom bayit,* and clearly the wife may continue to follow her own family's customs and her husband cannot impose otherwise on her."[28] A woman who wants to continue her own customs after she marries is no more attacking family values than is a man who maintains his own prayer *nusaḥ* in a new congregation is attempting to separate himself from the community. While one should normally continue to follow one's family's customs, wives have the option to change to the customs followed by their husbands. It is only to prevent irreconcilable arguments that halakhah steps in to impose a solution; and all such imposed solutions are inherently unfair. If the solution leads to *shalom bayit,* it would seem that not only can a woman continue to follow her family's customs, but there should be no objection to everyone in the family—including the husband—following her minhag. After all, there is no halakhic opposition to a person's deliberately moving permanently to a new community even though doing so would entail adopting the new community's customs for his own.

Even when a husband insists on his prerogative to have his family adopt his customs, he does not have absolute rights; he may not, for example, impose his personal stringencies on his wife. Writing to a man who objects to his wife wearing a wig without a kerchief, R. Feinstein rules:

> From the point of view of the law, you cannot prevent your wife from wearing [only] a wig. Though you wish to be more stringent, you cannot force your stringencies on her, as this is her business. Inasmuch as she is following the law of the majority of the *posekim,* which appears to be the halakhah, you cannot be stringent for her.[29]

Similarly, rules R. Halevi, a woman may follow her family's *niddah* custom of counting seven days even if her husband prefers that she follow his family's more stringent custom. His family's custom is not relevant.[30] And although a husband may insist that his sons follow his customs, R. Halevi agrees with the opinion that this does not necessarily apply to his daughters.[31]

In a way, this is similar to the halakhah that while both men and women are required to honor and fear their parents, a married woman is exempted from these obligations because she is responsible to her husband.[32] Rabbi David Mescheloff points out that this ruling is designed to deal only with an extreme case in which the spouses cannot come to terms in a conflict over the wife's giving allegiance to her original and her new family.[33]

> When life goes well, men and women can observe the mitzvah of honoring their parents even if it causes discomfort to the spouse and family, because they have a common understanding between them. In such a situation, there is no need for a halakhic ruling. Even if the situation becomes difficult and family tensions are created, wise men and women will know how to relate to the family's needs, to calm things down and perhaps let up on the intensive attention given one's parents.[34]

It is only in a crisis situation that halakhah must reluctantly step in to resolve the conflict. But when *shalom bayit* is the overriding family dynamic, a husband

and wife with similar attitudes toward their shared responsibilities have great latitude in developing strategies for creating a religious home life that reflects both their backgrounds.

The Family Meal

It is not surprising that the family meal at Shiloh was the setting in which Hannah found herself no longer able to tolerate Elkanah's misunderstanding of her distress. The family meal is in many ways a focus of interpersonal relationships. Both animals and human beings eat and then eliminate wastes, for example, but only a human can appreciate that these activities are part of a greater cosmic drama and therefore worthy of a berakhah (blessing). But even more significant than the fact that only humans can say a blessing before eating is the realization that only they can sit down to a meal.

This is not simply a tautological observation, an appreciation that only humans can conform to the complex rules of behavior that govern a formal dinner. A human meal reflects relationships between participants, an awareness that we can transcend our immediate selves, share and control ourselves even when we are hungry, and appreciate others even as we meet our own needs. This observation is incorporated in halakhah's insistence that a *seudat mitzvah*—a "mitzvah meal"—be part of every holiday and Sabbath observance.[35] Indeed, included in the formulation of the laws of seudat yom tov is the requirement that

> when one eats and drinks one must provide for the stranger, the orphan, the widow, and other poor people. And if one locks the door and eats alone with one's family, disregarding

> the poor troubled souls, then there is no *simḥah* [happiness] of mitzvah, but simply the *simḥah* of one's stomach.[36]

Participation in a human meal requires sensitivity to the physical needs of others and to our own spiritual requirements. Thus Rabbi Simeon ben Yoḥai maintained that if three ate at one table and did not share words of Torah, it is as though they had eaten of the sacrifices to dead idols.[37]

We take for granted that women share equally with men in this respect. Women may be formally exempted from time-bound mitzvot, but there is no exemption from either the meal par excellence in the halakhic tradition, the Passover Seder, or the rituals associated with the more mundane daily meals. Throughout the year, we educate girls to wash before eating and say *ha-motzi* (the blessing over bread at the beginning of the meal) and *birkhat ha-mazon* (the "grace" after meals), just as we educate boys. On Shabbat, men and women sing zemirot together oblivious to the fact that a generation ago R. Weinberg had to pen a responsum to justify the phenomenon. Boys and girls are quizzed on their week's studies and are expected to deliver *divrei Torah.* Both parents share equally in the adult Torah discussion, offering insights, posing questions, and suggesting answers.

Since we take all this for granted, it might be instructive to consider our reaction to women at the meal participating in *mayim aḥaronim,* the quick washing of the hands that often precedes saying *birkhat ha-mazon.* Someone who had not seen many women do this might interpret it as a protest of sorts, something to be attacked in favor of defending current traditional practice. But if we adopted this attitude, we would be acting in the tradition of Eli, confusing a form with which we were not familiar with a practice that we should oppose.

The original source of the custom of *mayim aḥaronim* is talmudic, an expression of concern that a harmful salt, *melaḥ Sedomit,* be washed off before ending the meal.[38] The danger of *melaḥ Sedomit* is no longer current, and, as Tosafot, Tur, and Shulḥan Arukh note, many people no longer end the meal by washing their hands with *mayim aḥaronim.*[39]

Quite naturally, women were never exempted from the practice of protecting themselves by washing off the *melaḥ Sedomit.* The alternative source for *mayim aḥaronim*—that one must "be holy" and wash one's hands before reciting the berakhah[40]—similarly applies equally to men and women. Thus, for example, Rabbi Moshe Sternbach, vice president of the "ultra-Orthodox" Eidah Hareidit, recently wrote: "I have found no basis for distinguishing between men and women [in this matter] . . . and it is obvious that [the obligation in regard to *mayim aḥaronim*] applies to women as it does to men. Indeed, I have seen that among the most pious people women do so."[41]

I suspect that the sociological explanation of why some women do not make use of *mayim aḥaronim* is that this ritual is often associated with the zimmun, the "call" to *birkhat ha-mazon,* to which we shall shortly turn. In many homes, *mayim aḥaronim* is brought to the table only when *birkhat ha-zimmun* is said. As many women mistakenly believe that they do not participate in the zimmun, they pass along the dish or cup without washing.

This is inappropriate in all respects. If the men are saying *birkhat ha-zimmun,* the women too are obligated to participate. And, in any event, *mayim aḥaronim,* independent of any connection with the zimmun, is equally obligatory on men and women alike. There certainly is no logic to their not participating if the men at the table do. In fact, the onus for explaining is more rightfully placed on the woman who declines to use the *mayim aḥaronim* than on the one who participates. Here is a case where "traditionalists" should be pressing women to undertake a neglected ritual rather than discouraging those who would opt for participation.

Indeed, the logical inconsistency of those who oppose women taking on observances from which they are exempted pervades the deliberations on women's issues. When we see something that we recognize, we assume it must be universally accepted; when we see something foreign, we jump to the conclusion that it must be opposed. We take it for granted that women will join the men in the sukkah, yet somehow are surprised when a woman uses *mayim aḥaronim*. What is often missed is that there is no requirement for women to sit in the sukkah, whereas there is no reason to exempt them from *mayim aḥaronim*.

Some people try to withdraw from the argument by taking a position like the one articulated by Rabbi Moshe Eisemann, the Mashgiach of Ner Israel Yeshiva: "Why not just tell the truth . . . [and] make a powerful statement that we refuse to tinker with our traditions, that we want our daughters, as far as possible, to be like our mothers and like their mothers before them?"[42]

Now, there is a Jewish community that truly wants its daughters to be like their mothers and grandmothers, but it is not the "yeshiva world" associated with Agudath Israel; it is the world of Satmar Hasidism. In the latter community, the Torah education of women has not changed much over the generations. But few of the grandmothers of R. Eisemann's contemporaries attended seminaries as do their great-granddaughters; few were fluent in Ḥumash and its commentators; few headed Torah institutions.

The Torah authorities of the *yeshiva velt* could have insisted on an educational system for women similar to the one in effect for generations, just as Satmar did. But they did not, because they too have had to come to terms with a new perception of women and their place in society. They have already accepted revolutionary developments like advanced Torah study for women as the *desired* norm, and it would be nonsense to suggest that this is not a reaction to the very forces against which they publicly protest. Indeed, when Agudath Israel justified the lack of Talmud study in its schools, it maintained that without Talmud study, its forty-five Beth Jacob high schools and dozens of seminaries have successfully produced both "contented housewife-mothers and teachers, and upward-mobile chemists, lawyers and physicians."[43] As if producing women who were upwardly mobile chemists, lawyers, and physicians had been the goal of past generations of Orthodox schools.

Nonetheless, these leaders are reluctant to approach this issue forthrightly and openly, perhaps out of fear that public discussion will accelerate a process with which they are not at all in sympathy. We, however, candidly discuss our new social reality, and have no trouble in saying, for example, that we expect women to be part of the total decision-making process in their homes, and that we assume that they will be full participants in the family's religious life.

Let us, therefore, gauge our reaction to a custom

cautiously emerging in some modern religious homes. The thought of a Friday night meal usually evokes the image of the father saying Kiddush—so much so that a generation ago women who were single or whose husbands were away would often go to "hear Kiddush" at a neighbor's home (and, contrary to halakhah, would have passed up saying Kiddush or Havdalah if they were alone, since they had been brought up to see these as a man's obligations). Today, of course, such women simply say it themselves. Interestingly, there is now an increasing number of families where the father's Kiddush is followed by the mother's saying *ha-motzi* over the two challot.

Her performing a ritual traditionally performed by the man of the house is hardly an arrogant attack on basic family values; it is rather a concrete expression of an attitude that most of us take for granted all week long. The halakhic logic is that *ba'al ha-bayit botze'a,* the head of the household generously distributes the bread at the opening of the meal. In a household of shared responsibilities and authority, the wife too qualifies under the rubric of *ba'al ha-bayit.* No one gives a second thought if a family guest, when leading the zimmun (the formal call to say *birkhat ha-mazon*), says, *bi-reshut ba'al ha-bayit u-ba'alat ha-bayit nevarekh* . . . ("with the permission of the master and mistress of the house, let us bless . . ."). Indeed, in some homes, the failure to include the wife will itself cause eyebrows to be raised.

The two loaves of *leḥem mishneh* bread that are required for the Shabbat meal commemorate the double portion of manna the Jews miraculously received before each Shabbat while in the desert. Authorities disagree as to why women share the obligation to partake of *leḥem mishneh.* (It may be because women too participated in the miracle of the manna;[44] or because *no* positive rabbinic mitzvah carries the exemption for women that time-bound Torah mitzvot do;[45] or because the preceding exemption does not apply to *any* positive Shabbat mitzvah.[46]) But they agree that women are equally obligated and therefore that all present can fulfill their own obligations by saying amen after the wife recites *ha-motzi.*

This option, with which many couples are quite comfortable, most certainly does not imply any intention to destroy traditional family images by, say, having the husband light candles or the wife recite Kiddush. Whatever the halakhic validity of such an interchange of roles, most of us have no real interest in rearrangements of this kind. But the *ha-motzi,* which has been—from a functional but not a theoretical perspective—an appendage to the Kiddush, was apparently ripe for development as a concrete expression of the current perception of the modern religious woman as a coequal head of the household. Not all families are interested in this change. But openness to such developments characterizes—or should characterize—our religious community.

The Zimmun

Whatever one's reaction to modifying women's participation at the beginning of the meal, there should be little opposition to including them in the closing ceremony. Indeed, here is another case where halakhah pushes us to *change* the current practice. It is worth looking at the sources in some detail.

One of the formal ways of expressing the idea that those who eat together have transcended their individual identities is the zimmun, the "call" to say *birkhat ha-mazon.*

"Three who ate as one," says the Mishnah, "are required [to say] the zimmun."[47] It is amusing in a way to hear the responses of principals of girls' yeshivot when asked why one of their students does not lead the zimmun before the *birkhat ha-mazon* after lunch. The reply is usually, "We're not feminists here."

But in tractate Arakhin the Talmud remarks that "all [including women] are obligated in zimmun,"[48] quoting the baraita from Berakhot 45b: "Women recite the zimmun among themselves, and slaves recite the zimmun among themselves. But if a group of women, slaves, and minors want to recite the zimmun, they may not."

Rashi interprets this to mean that women are not obligated to recite *birkhat ha-zimmun,* but may do so if they wish;[49] Tosafot agree with this reasoning.[50] Tur, quoting Rosh, notes that it goes against the face reading of the text in Arakhin, which seems to obligate the women; yet he accepts Rashi's interpretation in order to reconcile the text with the accepted custom in Ashkenaz that zimmun is not obligatory for women.[51] Bet Yosef quotes Semag's attempt to avoid doing violence to the literal meaning of the text by interpreting the Gemara in Arakhin as referring to a case where the women ate with three or more men, and the Gemara in Berakhot as discussing a situation where three or more women ate together without any men present.[52] In the former case they are obliged to recite *birkhat ha-zimmun,* while in the latter case it is optional. (Tur argues that this was a practical way of reconciling the talmudic texts that seemed to suggest that women had an obligation to recite the zimmun with the then-current practice of their not reciting it.[53]) Shulḥan Arukh codifies this interpretation as the *pesak;*[54] however, the Vilna Gaon is among the later authorities who side with Rosh in requiring three women to say *birkhat ha-zimmun* even if they ate together without any men present.[55] (All agree that ten women eating together would not add the word *Elokeinu,* as that requires a quorum of ten adult men.)

Everyone knows what the normal response would be to a situation where Shulḥan Arukh says that reciting a text is certainly permissible even though it is optional, while authorities like the Vilna Gaon say that the recitation is obligatory. We would cover all bases and recite the text. Thus Ben Ish Hai writes that the women in a household should recite the zimmun when they eat together.[56] That the current practice in many homes is the opposite should be cause to ponder.

This is especially true when the fact that women do not regularly say the zimmun reflects not some ideal but rather an accommodation to an unfortunate situation. Mishnah Berurah suggests that the rabbis exempted women from saying *birkhat ha-zimmun* if fewer than three men ate with them simply because they felt that most women, due to lack of education, were unable to recite it, and hence making it obligatory would be unfair.[57] (Tosafot take it for granted that women do not understand the words of *birkhat ha-zimmun* when they hear them.)[58]

Why would parents or yeshiva educators want to enshrine a view that presumes that their young women are too ignorant to be able to recite the zimmun or cannot understand a berakhah just as a man might? Women's reciting the zimmun when they eat together is nothing more than a natural consequence of the new high standard of Torah education for women.

Whether or not three women are halakhically obligated

to say the zimmun, there is no doubt that they may if they wish. As we noted above, Shulḥan Arukh takes specific note of this,[59] as do contemporary halakhic guides for women.[60] If three or more men were present, the women would have to defer to them in forming the zimmun; in halakhah, obligation takes precedence over volunteerism, and the three men are obligated. The presence of one or two men eating with three women presents no impediment to saying *birkhat ha-zimmun.* Rabbi Shelomoh Zalman Auerbach notes that in such a case one of the women rather than one of the men should lead the zimmun, but the men should answer.[61]

We therefore understand why a women's zimmun is a regular phenomenon in modern religious homes when, say, parents eat with their son and two daughters. Young girls look forward to reaching the age of bat mitzvah, when they too may be counted for the family zimmun. (In Sephardic custom, two men can include an older minor boy in order to say *birkhat ha-zimmun.*[62] Similarly, two Sephardic women may include an older minor girl to form the quorum required for saying the zimmun.[63]) Certainly students in a girls' yeshiva high school or junior high school should be introducing lunchtime *birkhat ha-mazon* with the zimmun, as should those in a coed yeshiva in which the zimmun is said in small groups of those who ate together.

This is not to suggest that halakhah is egalitarian in this matter. While three men or three women may—or must—say *birkhat ha-zimmun,* two men and a woman or two women and a man may not. This might have been a technical decision that grew out of the difference in the respective obligations of men and women in regard to *birkhat ha-mazon.* For reasons that do not concern us here, doubt was raised as to whether the Torah obligation to recite *birkhat ha-mazon* applies to women as well as to men. (There is no doubt that women have a rabbinic obligation.) Shulḥan Arukh refuses to adjudicate the issue, ruling that it is matter of doubt whether the obligation of women in respect of *birkhat ha-mazon* derives from the Torah or from the rabbis.[64]

The zimmun is an expression of the existence of a halakhic eating fellowship, so to speak. Within halakhah, obligation plays an important role in creating any fellowship relationship. One can therefore understand an argument that would extend this doubt to the question of whether men and women may join together to form a quorum. Of course, such reasoning conflicts with the rule that men who eat only vegetables—and, according to some, minors who ate bread—may join to form the zimmun quorum even though they certainly do not have a Torah obligation to recite *birkhat ha-mazon*. Yet one could reconcile this by noting that even if these men do not have a Torah obligation, theoretically they could in time acquire one, something not necessarily true of women.

The Mishnah rules that "women, slaves, and children—one does not recite the zimmun with them."[65] Despite this, Tur quotes a ruling of R. Yehudah ha-Kohen that a woman may join two men to complete the quorum necessary for reciting *birkhat ha-zimmun*.[66] Since R. Yehudah was not a radical who would have cavalierly disregarded a statement in the Mishnah, some argue that his interpretation excludes two women joining a man but allows one woman to join two men,[67] while others maintain that he certainly limited this ruling to the quorum of ten required to add the word *Elokeinu* to *birkhat ha-zimmun,* but would allow a woman to complete the quorum of three necessary for reciting the zimmun proper.[68] These reconciliations, however, appear to be somewhat forced. A more plausible interpretation would be that of the Taz. He explains that R. Yehudah understood the Mishnah to mean that a woman may not lead the zimmun but may participate in it.[69]

Apparently, it was an original component of *birkhat ha-zimmun* that everyone present would fulfill the obligation to say *birkhat ha-mazon* by answering amen to the leader's berakhah. This would be possible only if the leader and the participants were governed by an obligation of the same degree. Since there is doubt whether women have a Torah obligation to recite *birkhat ha-mazon,* whereas men certainly have one, a man could not fulfill his obligation through a woman's berakhah. This would preclude a woman's leading the zimmun when a man is included. Hence Taz's interpretation of the Mishnah: all may participate in forming the quorum, but because women, slaves, and minors do not have the same degree of obligation as men, none of them may serve as leader.

Of course, nowadays those present at a meal usually say *birkhat ha-mazon* on their own,[70] finishing each section before the *mezamein* (leader) does and thus being able to answer amen to the berakhot of the leader.[71] The function of *birkhat ha-zimmun* is simply to acknowledge the existence of the eating fellowship. Thus, if everyone present is saying *birkhat ha-mazon* individually, the only objection to a woman leading would be the traditional reluctance to allow (or encourage) women to assume public roles, especially in coed situations. This is not a minor point, but leading the zimmun is hardly as public a role as, say, being a yeshiva principal, something already sanctioned by our community and its halakhic leaders.

The Gemara states that women, slaves, and minors may not join together to say *birkhat ha-zimmun.*[72] Rashi explains that slaves were sexually promiscuous and suspected of homosexuality; allowing them to mingle freely with either women or minors would have led to immorality.[73] Based on this, Perishah to Tur cleverly justifies R. Yehudah's ruling by having him interpret the Mishnah to be a stronger version of the Gemara's prohibition: even with free men present, a mixed group of women, slaves, and minors cannot be put together for the purpose of creating an eating fellowship.[74] If the slaves are absent, it follows, there is no reason to exclude the women.

Yet it is hard to argue that fear of promiscuity is the real motivation of the halakhah in this regard. It is not simply that a woman may not join her husband and son—hardly a promiscuous situation—to say the zimmun. It is rather that when three men are present, not only is a woman's presence tolerated, but she becomes obligated to recite the zimmun.[75] And, as we have seen, a man may join three women who have formed a quorum.

Another reason offered for not allowing a unit of two men and a woman is that women have no *keviut* (regular unbroken attendance) at the table throughout the meal and therefore may not be recruited for the quorum.[76] Of course, we are generally not too exacting in regard to the "steadiness" of the men who may be recruited,[77] and, as we have seen, the women have enough *keviut* to be required to participate if three men are present. *Keviut,* however, is not necessarily dependent only on the subjective or objective circumstances.[78] *Keviut* apparently can be postulated abstractly by halakhah; when groups *should not* eat with *keviut,* they do not recite *birkhat ha-zimmun* even if they eat together.[79]

Mishnah Berurah ruled that "it is not pleasant" for a woman to join two men in forming a quorum.[80] Here too it is not clear whether halakhah is describing perceptions or prescribing attitudes. In past times, one might argue, a man might have been offended by the thought of a woman joining him to complete a formal religious subcommunity. Such an argument does not maintain that halakhah must adapt itself to the values of contemporary society. It simply holds that since halakhah itself originally intended only to reflect the frame of mind of the participants, then in this case, when those attitudes have legitimately changed, the ruling changes automatically. In the past, when women were assumed to be uneducated and illiterate, it would not have been pleasant to associate with them. Such assumptions are unwarranted in our religious community.

There is a principle that *kevod ha-beriyyot* (respect for others) is so important that it can at times take precedence over other halakhic prohibitions.[81] Thus, an ignorant am ha-aretz was originally excluded from the eating fellowship for the purpose of reciting *birkhat ha-zimmun,* but was eventually included so as not to cause disunity.[82] It would hardly be unreasonable to argue that this principle should be applied to our discussion.

In any event, we should note that there is nothing inherently offensive in not allowing a woman to join two men to form the zimmun quorum. The rule is fully reciprocal in that a man may not join two women to effect such a quorum. Halakhah, as we have seen, has no objection to men and women eating together; in fact, when they do so in large numbers, zimmun is obligatory for all present. Here, halakhah is expressing a concern that is well established and accepted within every Jewish religious community: sexual modesty.

Halakhah insists that, while coed situations are not inherently promiscuous, one must be aware that they have the potential to deteriorate as such. Therefore it suggests a subtle hesitation in forming the quorum, insisting that a coed situation in and of itself does not effect a change in the liturgy—in this case, allowing *birkhat ha-zimmun* to be said. But once the existence of a single-sex quorum has effected the change, the presence of members of the other sex is not objectionable in the least. Thus, when women join a situation in which the zimmun is obligatory, they become full members of the fellowship and share the zimmun obligation (and, according to Bah's reading, Ba'al Halakhot Gedolot would allow a woman to lead the zimmun[83]). When one or two men join a voluntary zimmun established by three women, they too may participate, as stated by R. Shelomoh Zalman Auerbach above.

We see in this discussion two important underlying principles. First, we must not do violence to the core value of sexual modesty. Second, the emergence of well-educated modern religious women not only demands that they have access to increased involvement in religious activities but insists that they undertake a commitment to be so involved. The home is the primary arena in which strategies for synthesizing these two principles must be worked out.

At Our Life-Cycle Celebrations

Simḥat Bat

Some twenty years ago, friends of mine made a Kiddush at their shtibl in honor of the birth of a daughter. The elderly rabbi announced the Kiddush and then, forgetting himself for a moment, turned to some of the older men who were sitting to his right and said (in Yiddish) in a somewhat bewildered tone, "They made a Kiddush as if it were a boy!" For a host of historical, sociological, anthropological, and other reasons, the birth of a girl was no cause for public celebration. This attitude is now changing, although not everyone is sensitive to, or appreciative of, the change.

Certainly it offends no one that parents would want to give the same sort of public expression of happiness at having a new baby daughter as they would "if it were a boy." It is therefore unfortunate that the discussion sometimes focuses on new "welcoming ceremonies," such as those included in The Second Jewish Catalog.[84] Their details include berakhot adopted or adapted from those said at a wedding, readings of various verses or Psalms, a ritual rupturing of the baby's hymen (to parallel circumcision), an ear-piercing ceremony (because all Israel heard the word of God at Sinai), or a ritual immersion in a *mikveh* (a symbol of women's sexuality).

The creators of these ceremonies are convinced that they are adding to *moreshet Yisrael,* the enduring Jewish tradition. "In the year 5844," wrote Sharon and Michael Strassfeld, "no one will remember, except as a footnote to history, the time when such ceremonies were not normative practice."[85] Not surprisingly, though, these new rituals do not appeal to the bulk of the traditional community. Halakhah recognizes and respects the religious creativity of Ḥazal (our Sages) and in a sense granted them copyright over the form of their system of berakhot. Within the tradition, creating new berakhot or saying established berakhot out of context is viewed as a desecration of God's name.

Circumcision is demanded by the Torah and has always been viewed by Jews as the symbol of Jewish identity. Rupturing a baby girl's hymen on the suggestion of a creative individual, even if it is medically benign, is nothing but a battery. One need not take sides in the debate about whether immersing a baby in a *mikveh* is but a mimicking of baptism[86] or, as the Strassfelds maintain, simply an extension of Meiri's view that when Abraham circumcised himself and thus entered the *berit,* Sarah immersed herself in the *mikveh* so as to also enter the covenant. Within the halakhic community, a *berit* milah has significance because it is a biblical command, not because it is a "meaningful ritual." The most moving new ceremony can never attain that biblical association. Indeed, to some, innovative rituals are a by-product of the view that *berit milah* itself is only a "meaningful ritual"—a perspective that halakhists cannot help but find offensive.

It is of interest here to consider a personal anecdote related by Jonathan Sacks, Chief Rabbi of Great Britain and the Commonwealth.[87] Generally, when expressing gratitude for something that is good for oneself and others, one says the berakhah of *ha-tov ve-ha-metiv*; when the incident or news is good only for oneself alone, it is *she-heḥeyanu* that is said. The Talmud indicates that *ha-tov ve-ha-metiv* is said at the birth of a son. But Arukh haShulḥan notes that "at the birth of a girl, one does not make a blessing, because there is not so much rejoicing at such an event." When their daughter was born, R. Sacks and his wife were upset at not being able to say the blessing *ha-tov ve-ha-metiv,* as they had when their son was born. Of course, as a halakhically committed person, he did not have the option of saying a blessing disallowed by the system. But he was able to explore options within halakhah.

R. Sacks explains that Mishnah Berurah allows the parents to say *she-heḥeyanu* when they first see their baby girl, as this is the blessing said when one sees a friend after an absence of thirty days. On the other hand, Rabbi Nahum Rabinowitz, the Rosh Yeshiva of the Hesder Yeshiva Birkhat Moshe, allows *ha-tov ve-ha-metiv*.

What Rambam codified, R. Rabinowitz reasoned, was not a specific ruling that this blessing is to be said only at the birth of a son, but a general rule that it is said over something that is good for oneself and for others. The Talmud gave only a specific example, valid in its own time. Since not everyone could be assumed to take delight in the birth of a daughter, the Talmud ruled that the blessing not be said. But Rambam codified the rule, not the example. Thus, R. Rabinowitz concluded, applying the rule here and noting the joy of the parents, it becomes obvious that the blessing should be said. Arukh ha-Shulḥan, on the other hand, applied the principle to the reaction of most Jews throughout Jewish history, not the reaction of these individual parents.

R. Sacks related this incident in the context of a discussion of creativity and innovation in halakhah. Who, he asked, was being more innovative? Mishnah Berurah, without precedent, transferred the blessing over a daughter—unlike that of a son—from the category of *birkhat hoda'ah* (a blessing of thanksgiving) to *birkhat re'iyah* (a blessing said on seeing specific things). R. Rabinowitz, however, placed the blessing over children in a more general framework and reestablished the connection between the blessing and the impact of the event over which it is made on the lives of those who would recite it. (Arukh ha-Shulḥan accepts this connection, but applies it to the community as a whole, not the individuals involved.) This debate is an interesting one, but what concerns us here is the legitimacy of searching and reassessing sources to apply them to familiar events taking place in a new social context.

In any event, to return to a "welcoming ceremony" for daughters, it is important to appreciate that it is not the ceremonial aspect of the *berit milah* that most parents want to duplicate. It is rather the *public attention* given the birth of a son that they want for their daughter. This need be nothing more than a Kiddush or a *seudat mitzvah.* For want of a better name, a public expression of this kind is often termed a *simḥat bat*; Sephardic communities have traditionally called it *zeved ha-bat.*[88] Many of the normative rituals now carried out in shul can be moved to this celebration.

For example, adopting the custom of the *zeved ha-bat* to the *simḥat ha-bat* would make it possible for the baby to be named at a family and communal affair—something that was certainly the original intention of naming during the Torah reading, but which gets lost when contrasted with the setting for a *berit milah.* There seems to be no reason to exclude women from announcing the name, either at a *simḥat bat* or a *berit milah* (where a woman would say *kayem et ha-yeled*). This would also be a suitable time for the mother to say a devar Torah and—if it has not yet been done in shul—to recite *birkhat ha-gomel* (a topic to which we shall turn below) as well as *birkhat she-heḥeyanu* or *ha-tov ve-ha-metiv,* perhaps doing so *al ha-kos* (over a glass of wine). This would be fitting at a *berit milah* too.

A *seudat mitzvah* ends with *birkhat ha-mazon.* At a *berit milah,* a series of *Ha-raḥaman* paragraphs is added, and friends and relatives are honored by being asked to recite individual ones aloud. It might appear that these paragraphs are being interpolated into *birkhat ha-mazon,* but they actually follow the conclusion of the four berakhot, as do the "regular" *Ha-raḥaman* paragraphs recited daily and on Shabbatot. These paragraphs are not part of the canonized liturgy; there is much license for individual creativity here. There is nothing wrong with composing appropriate paragraphs for a *simḥat bat* or any other occasion, and, given the fact that we take for granted that women can read and speak Hebrew as well as men, it is quite natural to honor a woman with saying one of the traditional paragraphs at a *berit,* just as one might honor a man. This is the right place to make sure that we can hear the voice of modern Jewish women.

It is also a perfect opportunity for the mother to recite *birkhat ha-gomel,* the blessing said when one has survived a threatening illness or a dangerous situation. *Birkhat ha-gomel* must be said publicly in the presence of a minyan and two *talmidei ḥakhamim.* Generally it is said while the Torah is being read, but that is not a sine qua non for its recitation.

Because the berakhah is usually said during the Torah service in the synagogue, it has become customary for the husband to receive an aliyah and recite the berakhah "for" his wife following her recovery from childbirth. Yet, as Rabbis Moshe Sternbach and Ovadiah Yosef point out, it is a long-standing custom in the most Orthodox synagogues in Jerusalem for a mother recovered from childbirth to recite *birkhat ha-gomel* for herself, either from the women's section of the synagogue when the Torah is read or at a specially convened public celebration at home.[89]

It is instructive to note R. Yosef's quick dismissal of possible objections to her doing so. The fact that she might still be *niddah* after childbirth is irrelevant; *niddah* status is no impediment to entering the synagogue or reciting berakhot. There is nothing immodest in a woman reciting a berakhah publicly because the halakhah requires that the berakhah be said in the presence of a minyan. There is no issue of *kol ishah* or sexual arousal because the Shekhinah Herself is in attendance with the minyan, and there is no sexual arousal in the company of the

Shekhinah. Indeed, "the evil inclination is not to be found for such a brief matter . . . especially nowadays, when women regularly go out to public places among men."[90] Originally, women could be called to the Torah; the reason they are no longer is *kavod ha-tzibbur,* not fear of arousal or *kol ishah.* Thus, he concludes, "everyone concedes (*lekhol hadeiot*) that a woman may say *birkhat ha-gomel* in this manner."[91]

Parenthetically, for R. Yosef's ruling to be fully appreciated, it should be considered against the background of his specially prepared women's siddur, *Or va-Derekh.*[92] There is a long-standing debate between Ashkenazic and Sephardic halakhists regarding the blessings said by women before performing time-bound mitzvot from which they have been exempted. Basically, Sephardic *posekim,* led by Rambam (Maimonides), felt that one may not say the phrase "who has commanded us (*ve-tzivanu*)" regarding a mitzvah one is not obligated to perform. Sephardic women therefore perform these mitzvot without saying the introductory berakhah. Ashkenazic *posekim,* led by Rabbenu Tam, interpreted the phrase as referring to the general commandment to observe mitzvot and therefore allow women to precede the performance of these mitzvot with the same blessing said by men.

Ḥakham Ovadiah, however, posits a broader interpretation of the Sephardic position. Contrary to the general practice, he held that the rule prohibiting Sephardic women from saying a berakhah associated with a time-bound mitzvah from which they are exempted extends even to blessings that do not include the phrase *ve-tzivanu.* In particular, because women are exempted from saying Pesukei de-Zimra and Keriat Shema, they may not say the traditional berakhot in the siddur that precede and follow these texts. Accordingly, God's name is omitted from the opening and closing phrases of these prayers in R. Ovadiah's *Siddur Or va-Derekh* so that halakhically they lose their status as berakhot.

Similarly, the siddur includes a note explaining that women are exempt from praying Musaf, as it too is a time-dependent mitzvah. Hence, the user of the siddur is advised that it would be better to simply hear the ḥazzan recite the prayer when he repeats the Amidah. Generally, Sephardim say the opening and closing berakhot of Hallel only when reciting the full Hallel. When "Half Hallel" is recited, neither the opening nor the closing berakhah is said. These general instructions are included in R. Yosef's women's siddur, but a short note continues that women should not say the berakhah for Hallel on any day except the night of Passover. The opening berakhah is omitted from the siddur completely, and God's name is omitted from the closing blessing.

Yet, despite all this, R. Yosef enthusiastically endorses the public recitation of *birkhat ha-gomel* by women. Certainly most people would regard women praying Musaf as less disruptive of contemporary halakhic practice than a woman's reciting *birkhat ha-gomel* in shul (and most congregations would hardly consider adopting this siddur). But just as he cannot bring himself to permit what he feels others have mistakenly allowed, R. Yosef must support what he believes is actually permitted.

In any event, one would be hard-pressed to find an argument against a woman's saying *birkhat ha-gomel* aloud in shul instead of having her husband say it for her. Indeed, reciting it at a *berit* or a *simḥat bat* seems most appropriate.

Bat Mitzvah

Even more popular than the *simḥat bat* celebration when a girl child joins the Jewish community is the bat mitzvah celebration when a young woman becomes an adult. Of course, there is nothing particularly modern about celebrating a girl's reaching the age of mitzvot. The principle that "it is better to act out of halakhic obligation rather than personal commitment" applies to women as well as to men. A religious girl should feel no less excited than a boy about finally being obligated to perform the mitzvot.

Certainly, when we see women as full members of the Torah community—much as we take for granted their full membership in our everyday society—it becomes difficult to oppose the logic of the bat mitzvah celebration. As Rabbi Yeḥiel Yaakov Weinberg notes, instituting bat mitzvah celebration is but a logical extension of the relatively recent establishment of serious Torah schools for women.

> Straight logical reasoning and the basic principles of pedagogy just about compel us to also celebrate girls reaching the age of obligation in mitzvot. The distinction that we maintain between boys and girls celebrating the reaching of maturity deeply offends the personal feelings of the mature girl, who in other areas of life has already earned emancipation, as it were.[93]

R. Weinberg then raises the more general issue of the limits that should govern the establishment of ceremonies that seem to imitate those of the non-Jewish world. He concludes that any similarities between a bat mitzvah celebration and, say, Christian confirmation ceremonies are irrelevant. "As a practical matter, the issue turns on the motivation of those who wish to introduce the innovation of a bat mitzvah celebration, on whether they are acting *le-shem mitzvah* or to imitate the non-Jewish world."[94]

Bat mitzvah celebrations in our religious community are conducted *le-shem mitzvah.* The problem, then, is how to concretize our natural inclination in this area. There is nothing particularly constraining about Rabbi Moshe Feinstein's insistence that any ceremony be kept out of the synagogue service.[95] A bar mitzvah is—or should be—the celebration of the boy's becoming obligated in mitzvot; the Torah reading is but his first opportunity to perform certain mitzvot publicly. As women do not read from the Torah during a regular synagogue service, we are naturally directed outside the prayer service to celebrate a girl's becoming a bat mitzvah.

Of course, some parents are concerned only with the public show and do not see the obligation in mitzvot as something to celebrate. The key, then, for understanding the parents' motivation in organizing a bat mitzvah party is in how they celebrate their daughter's coming of age and taking on the obligation of performing the mitzvot, there being no public synagogue Torah reading or the like. Local rabbis should take the lead in working out a proper observance. Certainly their relative inaction has nothing to do with enforcing traditional values.

The form that the bat mitzvah celebration takes should reflect our perspective on women's role in society. In our schools, we educate girls to demonstrate their maturity with a public performance of some kind; they learn to speak in front of their respective classes, give reports, hold school office, and so on. Our religious expression should take note of this widespread practice, and we should expect the bat mitzvah girl to present herself in some way as an adult. The devar Torah is a natural vehicle for this public adult performance; hence the growing custom of the girl's *siyyum* being the center of a bat mitzvah celebration. Some girls will finish a massekhet of mishnayot, some a chapter of Talmud, others a book of Tanakh. (After all, not all bar mitzvah boys do the same thing in shul.)

Perhaps a technical case could be made for allowing a woman—here the bat mitzvah—to deliver a *siyyum* from the pulpit during a break in regular Shabbat services or immediately after their conclusion. The sermon is not part of the tefillah; we might simply reason that a woman may speak, if allowed to do so, from the same place as a Wednesday night lecture held in the shul. However, we have no real interest in further emphasizing the synagogue service as the main focus of Jewish life.

If we believe that reaching the age of mitzvot is equally significant for boys and girls, we should be careful not to send a contradictory message. For example, if the girl does not speak from the pulpit, neither should the bar mitzvah. The youngster's devar Torah is not part of the service and could be delivered elsewhere. The rabbi would certainly want to congratulate the bar or bat mitzvah from the pulpit, but if a girl is not called forward to receive a gift, neither should a boy. The simplest solution would be to arrange a seudah and preface it with a *siyyum*. This would also be a good opportunity for the rabbi to speak and present the synagogue's gifts.

A set of books would be appropriate for both a bar and a bat mitzvah. The candlesticks that some congregations give a bat mitzvah are somewhat impractical—most young girls do not follow the Lubavitch custom of lighting Shabbat candles—and involve halakhic problems.[96] When we think about it calmly, we realize that the real preference should be a Kiddush cup; the bat mitzvah is now obligated to recite Kiddush just as is an adult man.[97] In many homes, only the *ba'al ha-bayit* says Kiddush on Friday night; yet the sons at the table often have their own Kiddush cups as symbols of their adulthood. The same should be true of the daughters in the family who have reached the age of mitzvot.

While a seudah can be arranged for any convenient time, the seudah shelishit on Shabbat afternoon has the added advantage of being a community affair not limited to invited guests. Others have decided to make use of community Ongei Shabbat held in the synagogue complex after dinner on Friday night. A seudah on a Sunday for invited guests is similarly appropriate. Halakhists might disagree as to whether a meal in honor of a bat mitzvah is in and of itself a *seudat mitzvah.* But, as R. Ovadiah Yosef points out, when the meal is accompanied by appropriate *divrei Torah,* all must concede its status as a *seudat mitzvah.*[98]

Our yeshivot have a responsibility to educate their students in the meaning of attaining the age of mitzvot without encouraging the excess all too frequently associated with bar and bat mitzvah celebrations. School bulletins and synagogue newsletters should regularly congratulate benot mitzvah just as they do benei mitzvah. But group celebrations rob each celebrant of being the appropriate focal point for the day.[99] An appropriate model would be a breakfast for the girls' class following tefillot; the bat mitzvah (or benot mitzvah) can speak, as can the teacher, and the girl can be the focus of a simple *seudat mitzvah.* This same breakfast model would work well for benei mitzvah too.

A major technical halakhic issue associated with bat mitzvah celebrations is that of the berakhah *she-petarani me-onsho shel zeh* ("who has relieved me of this one's punishments"), usually said by the father of a bar mitzvah when the latter first gets an aliyah to the Torah. There are two long-standing debates concerning this berakhah as it is applied to a bar mitzvah: What does the blessing mean? and, Should it be said in full berakhah form (*be-shem u-malkhut*)?[100]

The latter question evolves from the fact that this berakhah is not mentioned in either the Talmud Bavli or the Talmud Yerushalmi. There is a general prohibition against instituting new berakhot; hence the reluctance to assign full status to this one. Sephardic custom is to say it *be-li shem u-malkhut* (in a contracted form.) This is in accordance with the general Sephardic custom of limiting whenever possible the saying of a berakhah that is questionable in any way. Ashkenazic authorities differ among themselves; the Gaon of Vilna, for example, rules that it should be said as a full berakhah, while others sided with the Sephardic custom.

There are two interpretations of the meaning of the berakhah. The first relates to the idea that a minor child can be punished for the sins of his father. When the child reaches adulthood, the father gives thanks that he will be no longer be responsible for the suffering of his son. The second interpretation holds that the father is responsible for educating his minor son in the ways of Torah. If the son sins, the father is held responsible for his transgressions. Now that the son is responsible for his own education, the father gives thanks for no longer being held responsible.

As former Israeli Chief Rabbis Isaac Nissim and Ovadiah Yosef point out, both reasons apply equally to a girl who reaches the age of mitzvot.[101] They therefore rule that the father should say the berakhah be-li shem u-malkhut (following the Sephardic custom), when his daughter reaches the age of mitzvot.

Rabbi Elkayim Elinson notes further that this line of reasoning applies equally, not only to daughter and son, but to mother and father. Indeed, he points out, the mother may have a greater obligation than the father in educating a daughter. Preference, he says, should therefore be given to the mother at a bat mitzvah celebration (although both can say the berakhah).[102] Similarly, the mother can recite the berakhah at a bar mitzvah celebration too. R. Elinson cites Rabbis Nissim and Yosef to the effect that the berakhah should be said be-li shem u-malkhut, although it is unclear why those authorities who say that a full berakhah should be said at a bar mitzvah celebration would not maintain the same position for a bat mitzvah. Either way, just as the mother can say *birkhat ha-gomel* in the synagogue during the Torah reading, she can do so for this berakhah, although she might better recite it at the *seudat mitzvah* when she speaks. Here is another opportunity to have the mother's voice heard in our community, and it should not be lost.

Sheva Berakhot

There is a widespread custom of arranging special dinners in honor of a new bride and groom during the first week of their marriage so as to provide opportunities for the recitation of the Sheva Berakhot, the series of seven marriage blessings, after each meal. In modern religious homes, we already hear the woman's voice in the *divrei Torah* she often delivers. Moreover, there seems to be little reason to exclude women from reciting some or all of the Sheva Berakhot (if a halakhic minyan is present).

An indication of the level at which those opposed to this suggestion conduct their discussion of the issue may be found in Sova Semahot, a well-researched book on the laws of Sheva Berakhot.[103] The author records every available source on every related issue, noting also opinions that conflict with his own decisions. There is only one ruling that he records without citing any source at all. "It is *pashut* [simply obvious]," he writes, "that the law is that a woman may not recite these blessings."[104] However, an examination of the sources reveals that it is not *pashut* at all.

The Mishnah records the basic limitation on saying these blessings: "One does not say *birkhat aveilim* [the mourners' blessing] . . . or *birkhat ḥatanim* [the grooms' blessing] . . . with fewer than ten [adult free men present]."[105] This is not the only parallelism between the religious laws associated with the life-cycle events of marriage and death. The marriage celebration lasts seven days, as does the period of mourning. Both *birkhat aveilim* and *birkhat ḥatanim* are repeated throughout the week in the presence of a minyan, provided that someone who has not previously heard them recited (*panim ḥadashot*)[106] is present along with, respectively, the mourner and the bride and groom. But *birkhat aveilim* has fallen into disuse, while the laws of *birkhat ḥatanim* have evolved considerably, as we shall see.

The Talmud records the dictum of R. Ḥelbo in the name of Rav Huna that "anyone who takes pleasure from a marriage feast (*seudat ḥatan*) and does not cheer him [the groom] has a fivefold violation."[107] Maharsha notes that this dictum was the basis for Ḥazal's enactment of the seven *birkhat ḥatanim*; although there are many ways of cheering the bride and groom, the Sages decreed that it was to be done by reciting the Sheva Berakhot.[108] As anyone who takes pleasure from the feast is thereby required to recite the Sheva Berakhot, at this stage there seems to be no reason for excluding women from this obligation.

Radbaz ties the obligation of those who participated in the wedding feast to the more general ruling of Rambam concerning everyone's responsibility to the new couple.[109] Rambam rules:

> It is a positive commandment of the Sages . . . to cheer the bride and groom and provide for all their needs. And these are acts of kindness done by oneself and which have no set quantities. Even though all these mitzvot were promulgated by the Sages, they all fall under the rubric of "You shall love your neighbor as yourself."[110]

Here too there seems to be no reason to exclude women from this obligation. Nonetheless, Rabbi Shaul Yisraeli maintains that the mitzvah to cheer the bride and groom is not obligatory for women. And since he sees the recitation of the Sheva Berakhot as but one of the specific ways that the mitzvah can be fulfilled, they have no obligation to recite them.[111]

This position has serious consequences. In halakhah in general—and in matters of prayers and berakhot in particular—obligation is an important consideration. If several people are obligated to say a berakhah, they can all fulfill their duty by listening to one person recite the blessing. (This is regularly done, for example, on Friday nights, where everyone who is obligated to say Kiddush fulfills his or her obligation through the one person who recites it.) However, the requirement for using this procedure is that the person reciting the blessing have the maximum obligation of all those present. (Thus Shulḥan Arukh rules that because men and women have the same obligation in respect of Kiddush, a man can fulfill his obligation by listening to a woman recite the prayer.[112]) If all the men at the meal are obligated to say Sheva Berakhot and the women are not, a woman could not recite the blessings on behalf of everyone. And since a minyan of adult free men is required for reciting all seven blessings, there would be no possibility of an all-female audience whose members would share the same level of obligation.

Moreover, there is an additional difficulty regarding blessings. Berakhot are, in a sense, copyrighted liturgical forms that may be recited only for the purposes for which they were created. Thus, for example, one may compose and recite an original prayer of appreciation at the sight of, say, an orchard. But if one recites the blessing *borei peri ha-etz* without actually eating an apple, the berakhah becomes a serious violation instead of a positive religious expression. Thus if women are really excluded from saying the Sheva Berakhot, one cannot cavalierly allow them to do so.

R. Yisraeli's reasoning is as follows: reciting the Sheva Berakhot constitutes but one way of fulfilling the obligation to cheer the groom—and it is only the groom who must be cheered, not the bride and groom. One of the main ways of cheering him is to dance before him, and it would violate all laws of modesty for the women to do so publicly. They therefore are exempted both from the general obligation to cheer him and from any specifics of this obligation (such as Sheva Berakhot). Of course, men could dance before the groom while the women dance before the bride. But, says R. Yisraeli, there is no obligation on the audience to cheer the bride; that is an obligation that falls only on the groom. True, the Talmud asks, "How does one dance before the bride?"[113] That, he explains, is because it cheers the groom when people dance before the bride.

Yet with all due respect, the argument seems a bit forced. The obligation to dance seems to be built on the obligation to say the Sheva Berakhot, not conversely. Exempting someone from a duty to dance should not carry an exclusion from saying the berakhot. And even if we were to concede that there is no obligation to cheer the bride, R. Yisraeli recognizes that dancing before her cheers the groom. Thus, women have a sufficiently modest opportunity to fulfill an obligation to cheer the groom. Indeed, the Midrash notes that the dogs did not eat the soles of Jezebel's feet because she had used them to fulfill the mitzvah of dancing before the bride and groom, and Tur records this in its codification.[114] Moreover, Rambam clearly says that the mitzvah is to cheer the bride and groom. He sees this as part of the mitzvah of "loving your neighbor as yourself," and there is no reason to exempt women from the general obligation or from any of the other specifics mentioned by Rambam (to visit the sick, console the mourners, bury the dead, marry off brides, etc.).

Although the Sheva Berakhot seem to grow out of the response required of participants in the festive meal, if they are seen as a specific example of how to cheer the bride and groom, one could conceivably recite them out of the context of a meal. Indeed, several early authorities sever the tight connection to the meal, based primarily on Massekhet Soferim's comment that "It was the custom to say *birkhat ḥatanim* over a cup of wine in the morning and at night before the meal in the presence of ten [adult free men] and *panim ḥadashot.*"[115] However, as a practical halakhic matter, they are now said only after a meal, and the Gaon of Vilna emended the text to read "after" instead of "before," thus eliminating the primary basis for the earlier rulings.

Rambam, in fact, records the obligation to say *birkhat ḥatanim* in his discussion of the laws of *birkhat ha-mazon.*[116] After recording the general laws of *birkhat ha-mazon,* he notes (in halakhah 5) that the Retzeh paragraph is added on Shabbat; (in halakhah 6) that Al ha-Nissim is added on Ḥanukkah and Purim, and Ya'aleh ve-Yavo on its appropriate days; (in halakhah 7) that a guest adds his or her appropriate blessing; (in halakhah 8) that in the home of a mourner the appropriate blessing of consolation is added; (in halakhah 9) that *birkhat ḥatanim,* which he later defines as Asher Bara (the last of the Sheva Berakhot), is added in the home of a newly married groom; and (in halakhah 10) that if a minyan of ten (adult free men) is present and some have not yet heard all Sheva Berakhot, then all seven blessings are recited for them.

Most significantly, in halakhah 9, after noting that *birkhat ḥatanim* is added by the individual in *birkhat ha-mazon,* Rambam adds: "Neither slaves nor minors recite this blessing." This is a meaningful departure from his usual triad of "women, slaves, and minors."

Sefer ha-Menuḥah offers two explanations for the exclusion of these groups. The first is that they are excluded from uniting to form the group necessary for reciting *birkhat ha-zimmun*—the preliminary blessing to *birkhat ha-mazon.*[117] The second is that while women are obviously active participants in matters of marriage, slaves are excluded from matters of marriage and divorce (as are minors),[118] and therefore should not recite the extra blessing associated with a new marriage.

Clearly, the first explanation is deficient for several reasons. First, it ignores the explicit change in Rambam's language. Second, it introduces a concept clearly absent from Rambam's formulation. The discussion here is about a paragraph to be added to an individual's personal *birkhat ha-mazon* and in no way involves the issue of *birkhat ha-zimmun*. Unquestionably, the simple meaning of Rambam's ruling is that a woman may say Asher Bara as part of her individual *birkhat ha-mazon*.[119]

But Shulḥan Arukh makes an important shift in summarizing these halakhot.[120] Ten adult males must be present to say *birkhat ḥatanim*, whether it is said at the marriage ceremony or after *birkhat ha-mazon*. "If only the Asher Bara blessing is said after *birkhat ha-mazon*, the presence of ten is not necessary." Rema's gloss is that "but three are necessary"; as Be'urei ha-Gra explains, this is "so that there will be a zimmun." *Birkhat ḥatanim* is no longer simply part of an individual's *birkhat ha-mazon*; it is now dependent on the existence of a zimmun.[121] Indeed, in responding to the question of whether one may leave a wedding meal before the Sheva Berakhot are said, R. Moshe Feinstein rules that those obligated to hear *birkhat ha-zimmun* must hear the Sheva Berakhot, and the way to free oneself from the obligation of the latter is to exempt oneself from the obligation of the former.[122]

Most significantly, Shulḥan Arukh notes after this formulation that *birkhat ḥatanim* is not to be recited by slaves and minors, again not excluding women. Ḥelkat

Meḥokek explains there that the slaves and minors are excluded because they cannot be included in the three required for the zimmun. But, as we saw, women are obligated to recite *birkhat ha-zimmun* if they eat with the men, and have the option of doing so if they eat alone. Therefore they are not excluded from saying *birkhat ḥatanim*.

R. Shelomoh Zalman Auerbach notes that if one or two men eat with three or more women, the women may recite *birkhat ha-zimmun* and the men should respond.[123] (Neither of the men should lead the zimmun because together they do not constitute a quorum, and if one of them said *birkhat ha-zimmun,* it would give the impression that a woman was allowed to join them to complete the required quorum.) It therefore follows that if two women eat with the bride and groom, they may form a zimmun and add the Asher Bara blessing, which does not require a minyan. The author of Halikhot Beitah agrees with this conclusion but suggests that Asher Bara should be said only if the women actually exercised their option of zimmun.[124] An additional issue to be considered is that of *tzeniut* (modesty). In general, the tradition takes the view that a woman should not project herself publicly. In many circles, it would be considered immodest for a woman to deliver a Torah lecture to a group of men, let alone lead them in a blessing. Of course, many groups within the halakhic community are quite comfortable with women teaching men, assuming professional leadership in yeshivot (even though that entails working with male teachers and parents), working as doctors, lawyers, and the like. But this by itself is hardly sufficient to settle the issue.

We saw, however, that women can recite *birkhat*

ha-gomel publicly, either in shul at the time of the Torah reading or at a specially convened celebration. Some might feel that this is immodest behavior, noted Rabbi Ovadiah Yosef, Rishon le-Tziyyon and former Chief Rabbi of Israel, "but I say that the evil inclination is not to be found for such a brief matter . . . especially nowadays when women regularly go out to public places among men. . . . [Similarly, under these circumstances] one need not be concerned about the issue of *kol zemer shel ishah ervah* ['a woman's singing voice is sexually arousing']."[125] One cannot apply this ruling haphazardly, but it certainly seems to apply to our situation.

Thus the objection raised by Rabbi Moshe Halevi Steinberg to women saying Sheva Berakhot because of *kol ishah* concerns is not convincing, especially when he compares it to a woman saying Kaddish.[126] As we shall see when we turn to the issue later, that was not what troubled those who opposed women saying Kaddish. Indeed, R. Steinberg himself goes on to express his real concern: "If we allow women to say the Sheva Berakhot, it will be used as a precedent for other demands, including mixed seating in public prayer, as is done by Reform and Conservative [congregations]."

But this logic can be argued for the opposite conclusion, as did Rabbi Aaron Soloveitchik regarding Kaddish:

> Nowadays, when there are Jews fighting for equality for men and women in matters such as aliyot, if Orthodox rabbis prevent women from saying Kaddish when there is a possibility for allowing it, it will strengthen the influence of Reform and Conservative rabbis. It is therefore forbidden to prevent daughters from saying Kaddish.[127]

This argument has obvious relevance to Sheva Berakhot as well as Kaddish.

We may also briefly mention women's participation in two other areas surrounding the wedding before turning to the ceremony itself: Shabbat Kallah and the kallah's *tish*.

The Shabbat before the wedding is the usual time for the ḥatan's *aufruf*—the opportunity for him to be called to the Torah in celebration of his forthcoming marriage. Because many brides and grooms observe the custom of not seeing each other for a week before the wedding, the bride is often absent from the celebration, while the groom is surrounded by friends and family. It is no surprise, then, that this has given rise to a Shabbat Kallah—the bride's Shabbat,—either on the same Shabbat as the *aufruf* or the one before. The logic and appropriateness of this additional celebration is uncontestable.

At the wedding, the ḥatan is honored at a *tish* (literally, "table") while the general reception is proceeding. The groom's friends join him at the *tish,* singing, dancing around him, and offering *divrei Torah.* Meanwhile, the kallah very often sits on a "throne," surrounded by female guests admiring and discussing her and her gown. Not surprisingly, many a learned bride, offended by such ostentatious and immodest behavior, has organized a parallel kallah's *tish.* Far from being an attempt to mimic the activities of the groom and his party, this is an illustration of women coming of age as full members of the learning community. Here is a new opportunity for religious expression that should be encouraged by every *mesadder kiddushin.*

The wedding ceremony itself is a more complicated issue. On the one hand, there is no halakhic possibility for women to act as the formal witnesses. On the other, there is no more reason to exclude a woman from reading the ketubbah or speaking under the ḥuppah than there would be to exclude her from speaking publicly during the meal. Saying berakhot under the ḥuppah falls somewhere in between.

Rambam clearly allows a woman to recite *birkhat erusin.* In his formulation, this berakhah may be recited only by the person who actually performs the kiddushin: either the groom himself or the person he has appointed as *shaliaḥ* to effect the kiddushin.[128] Rambam specifically does not exclude women from those who may be appointed *shaliaḥ* for this purpose.[129] Nowadays, of course, this berakhah is said by the *mesadder kiddushin.* It should be said by the groom, but, as not all grooms are competent to do so, we demand that he appoint a *shaliaḥ* in order that he not appear arrogant[130] and embarrass those grooms who could not. Theoretically, as women are *be-torat kiddushin,* one could be appointed to recite the berakhah. However, as a practical matter, saying this berakhah is now an honor reserved for the officiating rabbi.

The status of the Sheva Berakhot said under the ḥuppah is a matter of some debate. As Rabbi Azarya Berzon points out, it could be argued that the seven blessings constitute either *birkhat ha-mitzvot,* in which case the obligation would be on the groom, or *birkhat ha-shevah* (or tefillah), in which case the obligation would be on the assembled group as a whole or the individual members thereof.[131] Either way, a good argument could be made for allowing women to recite the Sheva Berakhot. Since women are *be-torat kiddushin,* the groom should be able to appoint a woman as *shaliaḥ* to say them on his behalf. While women are unable to form the minyan required for their recitation, once the minyan is formed they too are obligated; hence, a woman present could recite them on behalf of the others present, as was the case with the Sheva Berakhot after the meal.

Yet, on a practical level, the argument may not be totally convincing. The public nature of a wedding ceremony (as opposed to the more private character of a Sheva Berakhot meal) is significant in that there is a general halakhic concern to delimit a woman's public appearances. However, there is a more important distinction to be noted here.

Generally, halakhah assumes that a couple living together want to create a halakhic marriage, and therefore, many halakhists would consider a *get* (religious divorce) to be necessary to dissolve even a civil marriage. But, in what must seem a strange situation to the casual observer, nowadays halakhah has a definite interest in undermining the halakhic standing of many marriages.

If a marriage is recognized as halakhically valid but the couple obtain only a civil divorce, the woman remains technically a married woman. Her second marriage is therefore halakhically adulterous, and any children from it are illegitimate. Given the high rate of divorce and the high percentage of couples obtaining only a civil divorce, the logic of the current mood becomes clear. There is no illegitimacy associated with a child born out of wedlock, as long as the marriage *could have been* contracted halakhically. Hence the current mood to invalidate Conservative and Reform marriages. Eugene Borowitz, a leading theologian and rabbinical leader of Reform Judaism, applauds this approach:

> I will gladly indicate on whatever ketuba-like document I sign that the rites to which it attests were not meant to create a halakhically valid marriage. . . . To me, such a practice

> would represent so slight a compromise of principle and so great a gain in Jewish unity that I would not hesitate to commend it to my colleagues.[132]

One of the factors that halakhically invalidates a non-Orthodox marriage is the double-ring ceremony.[133] Apparently innocuous in and of itself, the bride's act of giving a ring to the groom can be interpreted as casting doubt on the halakhic integrity of the groom's giving a ring to his bride. (Hence, when bride and groom intend to exchange rings, many Orthodox rabbis, in order to remove any doubt about the validity of the ceremony, make a point of either having the bride give the ring to the groom after the ceremony proper, just before the glass is broken, or of announcing that her ring is a gift while his was used to effect the kiddushin. The average wedding guest usually does not understand the purpose of such an announcement.)

One might argue that most egalitarian wedding ceremonies create a presumption of invalidity, basically because women may be asked to serve as witnesses. Therefore, this argument might continue, even though there may be nothing technically wrong in a woman's saying one of the Sheva Berakhot under the ḥuppah, we have a specific atypical interest in not creating an impression of egalitarianism during the wedding ceremony proper, a concern we do not have at a meal. Requesting restraint here represents so slight a compromise of principle and so great a gain in maintaining the halakhic integrity of the wedding ceremony that it seems appropriate.

Of course, the argument that technically admissible activities might be misinterpreted as being halakhically impermissible could be used against most of the proposals we have mentioned here—and, in fact, it is the driving force behind most of the opposition. While we should be sensitive to this concern, we must not let it paralyze us. A meal of friends and family is one thing; a public ceremony attended by a wide circle of guests is another. Drawing the line in theory may be subjective and complicated. However, it is often easy to see in practice on which side of the line a particular issue will fall.

In Our Synagogues

The Missing Meḥitzah

It is no wonder that Hannah met resistance and misunderstanding when she ventured into the sanctuary. Certainly our synagogues—our "miniature sanctuaries"—are the most difficult places in which to hear the emerging voice of contemporary religious women. As a halakhic institution, the synagogue is least hospitable to women's involvement. On a daily basis—excluding, perhaps, Shabbat morning—it is for the most part only men who congregate to pray, and any women who might attend are excluded from leading the services, getting aliyot, and so on.

Yet it is not necessarily their formal halakhic exclusion from leading the services that makes the synagogue proper less than hospitable to contemporary religious women looking for greater involvement within the greater community. It is rather the exclusionary tone of many of the synagogue's leaders.

Consider a shul in which half the congregants stroll in after the Torah reading, or one where once a month, two hundred people come for a lecture an hour before Minḥah on Saturday afternoon, and then, after the speech, a hundred of them get up and walk out, talking in the hall or going home to pray Minḥah privately. Of course, we would expect the rabbi to speak out—and not simply because of the requirement to pray with a minyan or to hear the Torah reading. It is one thing to pray Minḥah at home; it is quite another to be in shul and then leave to pray at home. It happens that people sometimes come late to services; planning to come late reflects something other than a halakhic judgment on the necessity of a minyan. A pulpit rabbi who focused only on the technical requirements here would have, in a way, missed the point.

Of course, in many Orthodox synagogues, this is exactly the situation regarding women. Virtually no women come to Kabbalat Shabbat or Minḥah; many arrive only for Musaf, despite the fact that they certainly have a stronger obligation to pray Shaḥarit. Women have an obligation to eat seudah shelishit, but are generally not to be found at the communal meal. None of this can be explained by claiming that women need to be home attending to young children or preparing the family's meals. Leisure time is a hallmark of most of our families, but even if older women may sometimes be busy, this same noninvolvement is to be found among teenage girls, who certainly have the time to participate. Is this attitude evidence that we are wrong in contending that the self-perception of Modern Orthodox women is undergoing change? Hardly. It reflects their keen understanding of the message being sent by the pulpit rabbi: Stay home!

Certainly a congregational rabbi knows that according

to many *posekim* women must pray Minḥah. Yet he is willing to look the other way when they walk out as Minḥah is about to begin. He will speak from the pulpit inviting high school girls to come to the shul's Oneg Shabbat, but does not suggest that they come to Minḥah on Shabbat afternoon and stay for seudah shelishit, just as they come in the morning to the teen minyan and stay for Kiddush. Young Israel synagogues, for example, take great pride in having made the morning service hospitable to women but are not troubled that the same women feel uncomfortable at afternoon services. There is no halakhic or hashkafic justification for this.

In some ways, too, the meḥitzah is part of this negative message. Not the meḥitzah in the main synagogue; men and women know that the meḥitzah is an integral part of the halakhic synagogue, and that it imposes certain unavoidable consequences.[134]

The negative message is to be found in the meḥitzah that is *absent* in the bet midrash used for daily services. Women are subtly being told: You may have learned to pray daily in school, but if you have the time and interest to join us in the morning, you'll have to make a public protest, not just walk in like the men. Of course, the women's absence—guaranteed by the absence of the meḥitzah—then becomes the justification for not installing one.

The disturbing consequences of continuing the current short-sighted policy are twofold. First, the synagogue and its rabbi become increasingly less important for those women who see their changing self-perception acknowledged and appreciated in other areas of life. Second, some of those who take prayer seriously will move out when they understand the message being sent to them.

Indeed, the establishment of women's prayer groups—a topic to which we shall soon turn—is nothing but testimony to the failure of synagogue rabbis and educators in general to fully address this issue.

The first challenge, then, is to take seriously the religious needs of women in the community and to make a commitment to enhancing their religious life. The question of whether women have a technical obligation to pray with a minyan is irrelevant to the claim that it is a *religious desideratum* for them to do so if it does not have a negative impact on their other obligations.[135]

Similarly, whether or not women are required to pray the formal Amidah a given number of times each day, they certainly should be encouraged to daven Minḥah daily. It is simply incomprehensible that a young woman who prays Minḥah every day in her yeshiva is made to feel that she is making some sort of protest by appearing in shul on Shabbat afternoon. There is no less reason to encourage young women to develop their religious sensibilities in the synagogue than there is to persuade them to cultivate their intellectual abilities in the yeshiva or seminary—something we all take for granted.

Second, we should address the challenge of increasing women's involvement in the synagogue proper without being frightened by the specter of, say, woman cantors, something clearly prohibited by halakhah.[136] Halakhically committed Jews have no trouble understanding that some things are allowed and others, which on the surface might look similar, are prohibited. We saw before that one would be hard-pressed to argue against a woman saying *birkhat ha-gomel* aloud in shul instead of having her husband say it for her. A woman who regularly attends Shabbat morning services should not be made to feel uncomfortable if she says *birkhat ha-gomel* from the women's section during the Torah reading.

A Quiet Berakhah

Sensitivity to women's increased participation in the synagogue might well begin with a modest adjustment in current synagogue practice, the ḥazzan's recitation of the berakhah *shelo asani ishah* ("Who did not make me a woman") aloud at the beginning of the public prayer service. There is no specific halakhah that this berakhah (along with *shelo asani goy* ["Who did not make me a gentile"] and *shelo asani eved* ["Who did not make me a slave"]) must be recited aloud; it is said quietly along with other berakhot (like *birkhat ha-Torah*) in all Sephardic congregations and a great many Ashkenazic ones. Nevertheless, this is a well-established custom in many synagogues.

Yet it seems that the berakhah should be said silently, like *birkhat ha-Torah*. The argument for this flows directly from the apologetic (in the classical sense of the word) for maintaining this berakhah against the protests of those who see it as an example of misogynist thinking. Judaism is not an egalitarian religion. Members of different categories—Kohanim, Levi'im, Yisraelim, men, women, etc.—have different halakhic obligations. There is no denying this and no changing it within the halakhic framework. Also basic to the halakhic approach is the principle that it is better to work under a sense of halakhic obligation than in a spirit of volunteerism. Hence, goes the argument in one of its many forms, a man is simply giving thanks for the fact that he is not exempted from the mitzvot from which a woman is exempt, just as a woman gives thanks for not being exempted from the many mitzvot from which a slave or a gentile would be exempt. (That this declaration is phrased in negative rather than positive terms is a stylistic matter that also has its justifications.)

Well, if that is the case, isn't it unseemly to give thanks for a privilege granted oneself in front of a person who does not have the same privilege? When women did not frequent the synagogue, there was no reason not to say the berakhah aloud. But now that women are there in numbers at the start of the tefillah, it should be said quietly, albeit appreciatively. To say it aloud in contemporary circumstances is akin to *la'ag la-rash* (mocking the poor) and analogous to exposing one's tzitzit at a graveside.

It is true that *la'ag la-rash* may be a technical halakhic category that applies only to the dead, who were once obligated to observe the mitzvot and no longer are.[137] But surely, whatever its technical status, *la'ag la-rash* is an ethical mandate: We should not embarrass people by making a point of noting in front of them that we have opportunities that they lack. This is a basic ethical demand. In any reading of the law, *la'ag la-rash* extends this concept to dead people rather than *limits* it to them. If such talk embarrasses the dead, so to speak, it *hurts* the living to be reminded of their lack of opportunity. It is true that if we are halakhically required to do something, we generally should do it even if it upsets others. But not when we are doing something that is not demanded of us by halakhah, as is the case here.

Arguing over whether this berakhah should be said aloud or silently might be viewed as either quibbling or evading the true problem of how to deal with a liturgical text that some find offensive. But the reactions to this modest suggestion are instructive. One, of course, was to deny that there was any issue worth discussing. Orthodox women, some argued, are not the least bit offended by the berakhah *shelo asani ishah*. If they are, it is only because they have absorbed anti-halakhic feminist attitudes. Indeed, for centuries women have not been hurt by hearing this berakhah. We should not be forced to accommodate in any way those who—perhaps innocently, perhaps deliberately—have been influenced by an anti-halakhic social environment.

This response is unsettling in so many ways. One cannot simply tell others when to feel hurt. Language changes. If once-benign words and phrases now elicit pain—certain examples in contemporary English come to mind—one should avoid them, rather than use them and argue that others should not be offended. Of course, we cannot extend this logic to changing a berakhah—but that is because there are halakhic constraints on changing *any* berakhah. We live with such constraints throughout our lives; it is the price we pay for halakhic commitment. But here there is no halakhic requirement to say the berakhah aloud.

More important, though, one should not be so quick to assume that Orthodox women have not been and continue to not be offended by this berakhah. Perhaps the best illustration of this is a recollection of Rabbi Barukh Epstein about his aunt:

> How bitter was my aunt, as she would say from time to time, that every empty-headed ignorant man, every ignoramus who hardly knew the meaning of the words and who would not dare to cross her threshold without first obsequiously and humbly obtaining her permission, would not hesitate to boldly and arrogantly recite to her face the berakhah *shelo asani*

> *ishah.* Moreover, upon his recitation of the blessing, she was obliged to answer amen. "And who can muster enough strength," she concluded with great anguish, "to hear this eternal symbol of shame and embarrassment to women?"[138]

This quotation is all the more poignant when we realize that R. Epstein was the author of Torah Temimah and the aunt he described was the wife of the Netziv, Rebbetzin Rayna Batya (daughter of R. Itzeleh Volozhniner and granddaughter of R. Ḥayyim)! A similar complaint, R. Epstein goes on to inform us, was made by the Rabbanit Sarah, wife of the Gaon Rabbi Yehoshua Leib Diskin. (Interestingly, this whole paragraph was omitted from the ArtScroll English translation of R. Epstein's book.[139]) Many similarly committed Orthodox women have the same reaction today.

It would indeed be a mistake to think that every such complaint is the product of contemporary feminism, though the latter might well be the stimulus for expressing long-felt feelings. For example, suppose a wife is very much bothered by her husband's pet name for her. For a variety of reasons, she never brings this to his attention. Finally, a friend convinces her to express her feelings aloud. It is true that her original hesitation might have been due to healthy or unhealthy reasons (or a combination of the two). And it is also true that her friend might have been nothing more than a troublemaker. But be all that as it may, once the husband knows her feelings, should he continue to use the name? The anti-halakhic stance of many feminists need not prevent us from conceding that they have brought to the surface many questions that need to be addressed openly and honestly. As Moshe Halevi Spero pointed out, "The inadequacy of . . . [various] rationale[s] for these three *berakhot shelilot* disturbed halakhic leaders long before feminist cavils popularized the problem."[140]

A third response is that of the slippery slope. Perhaps a good case for eliminating the berakhot can be made in this specific instance. But where shall we stop? As Rabbi Emanuel Feldman argues, "Should not one also be advocating a whispering of 'zokef kefufim' if a hunchback is in shul—he might well be offended by the berakhah (even though it has nothing to do with the human spine)."[141] And, he continues, should we not omit *pokeiaḥ ivrim* if blind people are present in shul? Surely they are hurt by our giving thanks in front of them for a gift they have been denied.

The simplest rejoinder is to note David Shatz's bon mot that one person's *reductio ad absurdum* is another's *in hakhi nami*.[142] If, indeed, we find that the hunchbacked or the blind are offended by what they perceive to be a cavalier insensitivity to their disability, then, absent any halakhic constraint, we certainly should stop saying the berakhah publicly in front of them. Actually, though, most people would not see these berakhot as analogous to *shelo asani ishah*. Conditions like blindness and being hunchbacked are disabilities; we are glad not to have them, and those afflicted with these handicaps would certainly prefer not to be. Surely we are not prepared to say that about femaleness. Many *posekim* hold that a blind person too must say the berakhah *pokeiaḥ ivrim*; it is praise for God's gifts to mankind as a whole. But in any event, we should not tell others that they should not be offended just because we do not see something as offensive.

In the end, the fear of the slippery slope is rendered irrelevant by our commitment to halakhah. It is halakhah that decides whether we may accommodate someone's feelings. Sometimes we are able to and other times we are not. It is no different from any other accommodation we make. If a guest asks us to change our menu and serve or omit a particular food, we shall certainly do so—provided there is no prohibition or obligation involved. It would never occur to us to say that accommodation is in and of itself improper. Why should it be any different in this area of life?

It is true, as R. Feldman has pointed out, that "slippery-slope legislation is an integral element of halakhah. The fear of the slope is precisely what lies behind *asu mishmeret le-mishmarti.* The concept of *asu seyag la-Torah,* of *geder,* of *gezerah,* of creating 'fence laws,' is that the Sages erect protective barriers to prevent us from slipping down the slope despite our 'commitment to halakhah.'"[143]

But it is also true that "we may not make up our own *gezerah* after the generation of the Geonim."[144] Making a "fence" can carry with it as great a danger as facing the slippery slope. It can prevent us from addressing serious issues—in this case, the need to correct an unnecessarily hurtful situation.

The fourth response is the most amusing and disturbing. We know you, its exponents say. You really want to drop this berakhah, but you're too smart to say so outright. This suggestion is all part of a plot to undermine the traditional view of women. Trick us into giving in here, even though there's nothing really wrong with your proposal, and we'll be at a disadvantage when you and your feminist friends come with the halakhically troubling demands that you really want to make.

It's easy to cry paranoia here, and even paranoiacs have enemies. It may be true that some enemies of halakhah might adopt such tactics, but living in fear of that possibility distorts and undermines. To take a historical example, the early advocates of Reform had many legitimate complaints; nevertheless, they deserved to be resisted because they were out to undermine halakhah. Two approaches emerged in dealing with them. One rejected any accommodation, including things we take for granted today in Orthodox shuls, like sermons in the vernacular. This accelerated a complete religious split and led to the development of an insular Orthodox community, leaving the bulk of Jewry devoid of a Torah life. True, when forced to choose, many people who flirted with Reform rejected it. But more chose the other way.

The other approach was that of the forerunners of Modern Orthodoxy, German Orthodox Jewry. Here, whatever could be addressed was done with gusto. When something was rejected, everyone could be sure that it violated halakhah, not an individual's sensitivities. As a result, we have not only Yeshiva University, but Ner Israel and other yeshivot as well. We have a community of benai and benot Torah fluent in the general culture and major players in the professions. Moreover, despite its public protests to the contrary, the bulk of the American Lithuanian Torah world has quietly adopted the approach of the Modern Orthodox community.[145]

As it happens, the question of saying the berakhah *shelo asani ishah* aloud did not originate with modern feminists. It was introduced more than a century and a half ago in Me'orei Or, a halakhic work written by Rabbi Aharon Worms, a disciple of the Sha'agat Aryeh, who served as rosh yeshiva, dayyan, and rav of Metz.

> It seems that we are forbidden to say *shelo asani goy* publicly, because it will engender hatred [among the gentiles]. And as to saying *shelo asani ishah* [aloud]—how can we publicly insult someone [*malbin penei ḥavero be-rabbim*]! It is enough to say [aloud] those berakhot mentioned in *Haro-e* [Berakhot 60b]; but who compels us to recite these three blessings [which are not in *Perek Haro-e,* but] in [tractate] Menaḥot [43b]? This can also be proven from the Shulḥan Arukh, which organized the berakhot that are to be said publicly in the synagogue in one place [Oraḥ Ḥayyim 46:1–2] and put these three berakhot in a separate paragraph [46:4]. While many siddurim place them among the [other morning] blessings, these [three] need not be said publicly. Thus the Shulḥan Arukh arranged [the paragraphs] as mentioned above.[146]

It is not surprising to find this reference dismissed with the observation that the Torah community has had many decades to evaluate the position of Me'orei Or and has found it lacking; witness the fact that his position was not adopted. Surely those today who do not favor changing the practice are no less sensitive and ethical than he was.

But this argument is anti-halakhic at best. Halakhah makes a point of recording minority opinions, and—as every reader of halakhah knows—they are often drawn upon in future years. In the years since the publication of Me'orei Or, until very recently, few women have attended daily services, few women have personally experienced the daily public insult conveyed by *shelo asani ishah.* A *posek* who hardly ever sees women in shul when the berakhah is read aloud would have little reason to hesitate about maintaining the status quo. But the very same *posekim* have never registered any objection to Me'orei Or's position, despite the fact that his work has been studied and commented upon by other *gedolei ha-posekim* over the years. Nowadays, Modern Orthodox rabbis see women in shul on a regular basis and personally notice the pain caused them by the public recitation of this berakhah. They should be taking the lead in adopting Me'orei Or's position that the berakhah should be said quietly.

However one recites it, the berakhah *shelo asani ishah* points to another difficulty, one that applies to the siddur as a whole and its implied inherent assumptions. Men and women recite different berakhot at this point in the service. In many siddurim, the blessing said by men is in regular type; following, in parentheses, is the blessing said by women, preceded by the instruction "women say." The message is clear: the siddur is meant for men; women are relegated to a footnote. This attitude is expressed many times over in the siddur. In *birkhat ha-mazon,* one calls for a blessing on oneself, and when appropriate "for my wife." The option "for my husband" is often not even mentioned.

New siddurim like Rinat Yisrael or the ArtScroll series are aware of the new social reality that finds women using the siddur as frequently as men. Again, it is not a newfound sensitivity to women, but an authentic response to a new reality. Women are now in shul; the ḥazzan, who represents the entire congregation, should not be saying aloud a blessing not said by a significant part of the *kahal.* Women are now using siddurim; the publisher should not assume that the user is a man. Men who learn to see the notice in older siddurim as negative may soon find themselves unwilling to announce, for example, that "Musaf on Simḥat Torah will begin when everyone in the shul has had an aliyah." In Orthodox shuls, about half of those present will not have had an aliyah when the decision is made to begin Musaf. That we sometimes do not notice this reality is in many ways more troublesome than our halakhic inability to provide the aliyah.

Women and Kaddish

Similarly, we should be comfortable with women saying Kaddish in shul. The origin of Kaddish as a basic mourner's prayer is somewhat obscure.[147] It praises God without mentioning the dead and is unintelligible to anyone who does not understand Aramaic. Yet its impact on those who grieve is clear and obvious. The obligation to say Kaddish speaks even to those who have distanced themselves from halakhic observance. A sense of duty to honor the dead with the recitation of this prayer prevails even among bereaved Jews who do not accept the theological premise that saying Kaddish brings benefits of one sort or another to the deceased.

Saying Kaddish is a response to death. Instead of resigning oneself to the sense of meaninglessness that accompanies a confrontation with death, one turns to tradition and its call to action. "Through the Kaddish we hurl defiance at death and its fiendish conspiracy against man," writes Rabbi Joseph B. Soloveitchik.

> When the mourner recites "Glorified and sanctified be the great name . . .," he declares more or less the following: No matter how powerful death is, notwithstanding the ugly end of man, however terrifying the grave is, however nonsensical and absurd everything appears, no matter how black one's despair is and how nauseating an affair life itself is, we declare and profess publicly and solemnly that we are not giving up, that we are not surrendering, that we will carry on the work of our ancestors as if nothing had happened, that we will not

> be satisfied with less than the full realization of the ultimate goal of the establishment of God's kingdom.[148]

What is the logic that would suggest that women might be excluded from saying Kaddish? Women have the same psychological response to death as men. Why should they not be offered the same traditional tools for responding? But such reasoning plays only a small role in the traditional assessment of this issue. Psychological insights must flow from the realities of halakhah, not conversely. The question of women saying Kaddish must be addressed through the sources and logic of halakhah, and not through current formulations of its ethos.

Yet it is the tradition itself that argues for allowing women to say Kaddish. Originally, writes Rabbi Naftali Zvi Roth, the mourner brought relief to the deceased by reciting Barekhu in his capacity as ḥazzan, thereby eliciting the congregation's praise of God in response. But not everybody has the ability to act as ḥazzan (or to get one of the few aliyot available on a Shabbat); minors in particular would not be able to exercise their responsibility toward their deceased parents. Therefore the early authorities enacted the saying of Kaddish after the recitation of Psalms, which is outside the formal prayer service, to provide an opportunity for those who would be excluded from acting as ḥazzan.[149]

This logic, of course, is easily extended to women. The argument is all the more compelling when we realize that the elicitation of *yehei shemei rabbah* in response to the Mourner's Kaddish is a form of *kiddush ha-Shem* (the public sanctification of God's name), a mitzvah for which women are fully obligated.

Centuries ago, Rabbi Ya'ir Ḥayyim Bacharach dealt with the case of a man who died leaving only a daughter and asked that a special minyan be set up to enable her to say Kaddish. He conceded in his responsum that the daughter's Kaddish brought *naḥat ruaḥ* (peace) to the deceased, that women participate in the mitzvah of *kiddush ha-Shem,* and that Kaddish could be said because a minyan of men was present. But in the final analysis he would not allow the daughter to say Kaddish, due to fear that an innovation of this kind might weaken allegiance to existing Jewish customs.[150]

It is important to be aware of the conscious effort here to separate the posek's social responsibility from his allegiance to the logic of halakhah. Ḥavvot Ya'ir makes no attempt to suggest that halakhah dictates forbidding the woman to say Kaddish. On the contrary, he rules that despite the apparent permissibility of her doing so, he must forbid it because of the danger that a permissive ruling might pose to the fabric of his community. Such a decision, of course, is by definition applicable only to a specific community at a specific time.

Thus, for example, Rabbi Yehudah Ashkenazi, the author of Be'er Heitev, comes to a different conclusion. He writes:

> In the responsa Keneset Yehezkel, the author [Rabbi Yeḥezkel Katzenellenbogen] wrote that it is specifically the son's son [who may say Kaddish], but the son of the [deceased's] daughter may not say Kaddish. And certainly the daughter has no Kaddish in the synagogue. But if they wish to form a separate minyan for her, they are permitted to do so. See there at the end of the section on Yoreh De'ah.[151]

In a similar vein, Rabbi Ḥayyim Mordecai Margoliyot, the author of Sha'arei Teshuvah, writes: "See [Rabbi Yaakov Reischer's] Shevut Ya'akov, part two, number

23 [should read: 93]: if he had only a daughter, she may say Kaddish [but] only in her house."[152]

There is a simple logic that explains the permissibility of setting up a separate minyan despite the fact that "certainly the daughter has no Kaddish in the synagogue." The underlying nature of the prohibition on a woman's saying Kaddish in the synagogue could not have been based on *kol ishah* or on the fact that women may not form the minyan required for the saying of Kaddish, for the same reasoning would also apply to the private minyan permissibly formed so that the female mourner could say Kaddish herself. However, the logic becomes clear when we realize that Keneset Yeḥezkel's responsum, which dealt with the question of who has precedence to say Kaddish in the synagogue, assumed a synagogue protocol different from our own. In most modern shuls, all mourners say Kaddish together. The original custom, however, was for only one mourner at a time to say Kaddish; when two persons both claimed the right, the question arose as to who had first claim. Keneset Yeḥezkel apparently maintains that inasmuch as a woman does not participate in synagogue activities, she cannot displace a man who wants to say Kaddish. Be'er Heitev sees no reason to extend this to a private minyan.

This ruling is all the more interesting when we note that the responsum of Keneset Yeḥezkel that he quotes specifically says (citing Ḥavvot Ya'ir): "If they want to form a separate minyan, they may do so for the son of the [deceased's] daughter or for anyone who wishes to say Kaddish for the benefit of the deceased, but not for any female whatsoever." Be'er Heitev apparently felt that Keneset Yeḥezkel agreed that *min ha-din* she could say Kaddish at home, but that she should not exercise this option because of the reservation suggested by Ḥavvot Ya'ir. Be'er Heitev felt bound by halakhah and not the policy advice.

If the reason for requiring a special minyan for the daughter is that she has no right to displace a man who has a right to say Kaddish in the synagogue, it would follow that in our synagogues (where the mourners saying Kaddish displace no one else), a woman could say Kaddish. In fact, this seems to have been the position held by Lithuanian *posekim* of the past generation.

In the early 1970s, when the issue came up in a chapter of Yavneh, the national association of religious Jewish college students, I asked one of the organization's leaders who was then learning with the Rav, Rabbi Joseph B. Soloveitchik, to put the question to him. Rabbi Ezra Bick (now at Yeshivat Har Etzion) wrote back:

> I spoke to the Rav about the question you asked concerning a girl saying Kaddish. He told me that he remembered being in Vilna at the "Gaon's Kloiz"—which wasn't one of your modern Orthodox shuls—and a woman came into the back (there was no *ezrat nashim* [women's section]) and said Kaddish after *ma'ariv*. I asked him whether it would make a difference if someone was saying Kaddish along with her or not, and he replied that he could see no objections in either case—it's perfectly all right.[153] Coincidently, checking around, I came across a number of people who remember such incidents from Europe, including my father (in my grandfather's minyan—he was the rav in the town). [Rabbi Chaim Yechiel Bick was the rav in Medzhibush in the Ukraine.]

Rabbi Pinchos Zelig Prag, gabbai of the Mir Minyan in Brooklyn, New York,[154] told me that one of the congregants, Rabbi Moshe Maaruch, who was born and raised in Vilna and who studied at the Mirrer Yeshiva, recalled that when his cousin died, leaving an adult daughter and no sons, Rabbi Ḥayyim Ozer Grodzinski allowed her to say Kaddish daily in the synagogue; another recalled that the Ḥafetz Ḥayyim had made a similar ruling.

Prof. Yaffa Eliach relates similar occurrences in her study of Eisheshok.[155] Tsipora Hutner Kravitz, wife of Rabbi Yosef Kravitz, recalled to Dr. Eliach that in 1935, when she was fourteen years old, her brothers were out of town when her father, Rabbi Naftali Menaḥem Hutner, the dayyan of the town, died. She said Kaddish at the graveside and continued to say Kaddish in both the new bet midrash and the shtibl until a brother returned. She recalled that at the same time Gitel Gordon, then eighteen years old, said Kaddish in the shtibl. Another former inhabitant of the town recalled that when the girls said Kaddish, they wore berets and stood in the men's section in the first row to the right of the amud.[156]

Rabbi Moshe Feinstein notes that "throughout the generations it was customary that at times a poor woman would enter the bet midrash to ask for charity, or a woman mourner would enter to say Kaddish."[157] Rabbi Yosef Eliyahu Henkin allowed women to say Kaddish in shul, provided they remained in the women's section.[158] He noted that in past times, when only one person said Kaddish, that person would stand at the front of the shul, something inappropriate for a woman. However, now, he continues, when all the mourners say Kaddish together from their respective places, a woman may say Kaddish.

Rabbi Soloveitchik also insisted that a woman saying Kaddish had to remain in the women's section. When, in the early 1970s, I asked Rabbi Gerald J. Blidstein (then a faculty advisor to Yavneh and now at Ben-Gurion University) about the issue, he wrote to me:

> The Kaddish matter is as follows. I was asked about the question last year, and looking into it, could find no reason beyond "general policy" for forbidding it. I spoke to Aharon Lichtenstein [then Rosh Kollel at Yeshiva University and now Rosh Yeshivat Har Etzion], who had the same reaction and said he would ask the Rav [Rabbi Joseph B. Soloveitchik, his father-in-law], which he did when I was on the other end of the phone. [Rabbi Lichtenstein] put the question to him, and then was directed to ask me whether the girl was stationed in the *ezrat nashim*. I, of course, answered in the affirmative, and the Rav then said that of course she could say Kaddish.

While European rabbis apparently did not always demand this, I suspect that the American *posekim* insisted on women staying in the *ezrat nashim* because they were concerned about the mixed seating that was gaining hold in many American synagogues. R. Henkin's opinion allowing a woman to say Kaddish in shul seems to be a lenient one boldly breaking new ground. Actually, it is a *conservative* opinion, for in opposition to some existing customs, it requires that the woman not enter the men's section to say Kaddish.

There is, to be sure, little reason to think that a woman who wants to say Kaddish is engaging in some sort of protest rather than simply attempting to use an acceptable halakhic form to deal with a real personal crisis. When a woman says Kaddish in shul (whether or not accompanied by others), it is analogous to her reciting *birkhat ha-gomel* aloud from the women's section. She offers her public praises of God and elicits a response from the congregation.

Yet in some quarters there is strong hesitation about acknowledging the permissibility of a woman's doing this. Consider, for example, Yesodei Smochos, a popular summary in English of the laws of mourning. Describing the graveside service, the author writes that following Tzidduk ha-Din, "the *male* mourner should recite the burial Kaddish."[159] Later, he indicates that during avelut it is the son who says Kaddish.[160] The source of the first *pesak* is given as Shulḥan Arukh, Yoreh De'ah 376:4, but the word "male" does not appear there. Five sources are given for the second—including the Kol Bo al Avelut—and the note ends (in Hebrew), "The daughter should not say Kaddish." In general, the author of Yesodei Smochos presents positions unequivocally in the English section but mentions alternative views in the Hebrew notes; here, though, despite the fact that the graveside is a private rather than synagogue service, the reader has no indication that some authorities allow the daughter to say Kaddish.

Kol Bo al Avelut is an encyclopedic collection of responsa on death-related issues. Here, though, the author knows of no source or custom that allows women to say Kaddish in the synagogue; it is *pashut* (simply obvious), he writes, that they may not. He is, however, willing to consider the question of a woman's saying Kaddish in a private minyan. He mentions Be'er Heitev quoting the opinion of Keneset Yeḥezkel that the daughter may not say Kaddish in shul, but omits the former's ruling that she may do so at a private minyan. The author quotes the permissive ruling of the Shevut Ya'akov but dismisses it as a lone opinion. "If she wants," he concludes, "let her go to the women's section in the synagogue and answer amen when Kaddish is said [by the men]."[161]

Another negative but much more candid approach is taken by Rabbi Shlomo Halevi Wahrman. He cites R. Henkin's position but cannot reconcile himself to it.

> I fear that if we allow daughters to say Kaddish as allowed by R. Henkin, then those of our contemporaries who are out to cause confusion—their aim being to create a new Torah and, God forbid, change our traditions, always looking for a high peg on which to hang their nonsense—will rely on this to count a woman in a minyan, saying that the most stringent have already allowed it.[162]

He then quotes a number of authorities who agree with him that the daughters should not be allowed to say Kaddish.

We have here an honest, unabashed public policy decision. There is no attempt to ignore the objective permissibility of a woman's saying Kaddish. Nonetheless, in this posek's opinion, more is at stake than personal sensitivity or reasoned halakhic analysis. Upholding the integrity of the halakhic system requires certain strategies; forbidding a daughter to say Kaddish is but one of them.

A similar approach is taken by Israeli Chief Rabbi Yisrael Meir Lau:

> As a practical matter, it seems we cannot rely on Rabbi Henkin's permissive ruling. Especially in our times we must be sensitive to the opinion of Ḥavvot Ya'ir. . . . Reformers might follow and draw the conclusion that women may act as ḥazzan. . . . Therefore we cannot allow women to say Kaddish in any way.[163]

Our feeling is that such a strategy—which can be used against any ḥeter in just about every area of contemporary life—is wrong, as forbidding what is permitted only encourages others to permit what is forbidden. Of course, one must appreciate the openness of this presentation; yet we must note that it runs counter to R. Feinstein's opinion that it is the woman's motivation in pressing for these matters that should advise our reaction.

This approach, widespread though it may be, might well be taken as a classic example of a strategy rejected by many. Maintaining the most stringent position, it asks committed Jews to reject, as much as possible, attempts by halakhah to accommodate itself to the standards of general society. Many people will find this position unacceptable, but the core group that accepts it will be able to maintain steadfast loyalty to the system and its leaders. Those who cannot accept these most stringent positions might indeed "fall out." But, on balance, those who proceed in this manner reason that the halakhic community will be stronger for it.[164]

But, of course, not all contemporary *posekim* take such a position. Realizing that forbidding what is permitted can well lead to permitting what is forbidden, Rabbi Aaron Soloveitchik writes:

> Nowadays, when there are Jews fighting for equality for men and women in matters such as aliyot, if Orthodox rabbis prevent women from saying Kaddish when there is a possibility for allowing it, it will strengthen the influence of Reform and Conservative rabbis. It is therefore forbidden to prevent daughters from saying Kaddish.[165]

The halakhic legitimacy of women saying Kaddish is unassailable even if not universally accepted. No woman should feel constrained from pressing to say Kaddish in her shul. If a rabbi feels that it is in the community's best interest to not allow an orphaned daughter to say Kaddish, he should make it clear that his decision is based on public policy considerations rather than halakhah. He should be confident that in a healthy halakhic community people generally feel bound by their personal halakhic authority. Additionally, many daughters will pass up the opportunity to exercise an option that all agree is not obligatory, finding solace in a more passive role. But a woman who regularly attends shul will feel resentment when she eventually learns that a meaningful, legitimate option was withheld from her. The rabbi, in his role as counselor, has an obligation to bring all legitimate options to the attention of the mourner.

Women's Megillah Readings

One of the more interesting developments in women's synagogue life has been the establishment of special Purim services where one woman (or a group of women) reads the Megillah for the other women assembled. Women who have studied the Megillah in class now have the opportunity to celebrate Purim together as full participants rather than simple observers and then attend a school *ḥagigah.*

The attractiveness of such a program for yeshiva-educated women needs no spelling out. It is therefore interesting to note the strenuous objections of *posekim* like Rabbi Menasheh Klein, who advises that

> if the women cannot get to the synagogue [to hear the Megillah read], their husbands can read it for them when they return or they can go to a neighbor. They should not make such a minyan, for in any event it has no value, as women may not be part of the quorum of ten required for a *davar she-bikdushah.*[166]

R. Klein mentions several technical objections to these women's groups: women may not read the Megillah even for themselves, as according to Behag they have an obligation only to *hear* it being read, and therefore cannot read it for anyone else; and even men can fulfill their obligation through another's reading if a minyan is present, and no such quorum exists in the women's group. But, of course, what motivates him is not the logic of the halakhah but his sense of the social reality.

> This is all a sinful suggestion of the evil inclination of the modernizers who would give women's groups the status and power of a minyan. It is difficult for me to discuss this, for it is pious women who would institute these new activities, which are against the Torah. and which our pure mothers and fathers never saw. The Yerushalmi notes that when men returned from the bet midrash they would read the Megillah for their wives and children. But we have never heard of women themselves making a minyan for this purpose. They should not try to be among those women who are taken up with the spirit of the times; they should aim to be like our holy mothers.

Needless to say, our pious grandmothers and grandfathers never saw women heading seminaries where women study the Megillah on an advanced level; we do not aim to recreate that reality. Having never seen advanced Torah study among women, it is no wonder that they never saw women gather to read the Megillah come Purim time.

Shulḥan Arukh rules that "all—including women—are required in the reading of the Megillah,"[167] adding that there is an opinion that a man may not fulfill his own obligation to read the Megillah by hearing a woman reading it. As a general rule, when Shulḥan Arukh gives a blanket (*stam*) rule and follows it with a dissenting opinion (*yesh omrim*), it is the first which is dominant—in this case the position that men may fulfill their obligation through a woman's reading, the position followed by the majority of *posekim*.[168] Out of respect for the secondary opinion, however, as a practical matter men fulfill their obligation through a woman's reading only in pressing circumstances. Rabbi Tzvi Pesaḥ Frank, late Chief Rabbi of Jerusalem, notes that this secondary opinion applies only to the daytime reading, not that of the evening, when a man may fulfill his obligation through a woman's reading.[169]

In any event, Mishnah Berurah concludes that a woman may certainly fulfill her obligation through the reading of another woman.[170] He suggests in a note that a woman may not read the Megillah for a large group of women because a public presentation by a woman is improper (*zila beha milta*).[171] We need not debate here the extent to which this concept has changed over time. Rabbi Shelomoh Zalman Auerbach maintains that the concept of *zila beha milta* simply does not apply to a woman's public presentation before other women, as demonstrated by the fact that, for example, women may clearly say *birkhat ha-zimmun* before a large group of women.[172] Thus Rabbi Alfred Cohen, himself unenthusiastic about women's Megillah readings, reports that they have the support of Rabbi Moshe Feinstein, Rabbi Pinḥas Halevi Horowitz (the Bostoner Rebbe), and Rabbi David Feinstein, as well as Rabbi Auerbach.[173]

Shulḥan Arukh rules that on both the fourteenth and fifteenth of Adar one should make every effort to read the Megillah in the presence of a minyan, and Rema adds that one must question whether women may join to make up the minyan.[174] Ran had argued that women must be counted in this minyan because they, like men, are obligated in the mitzvah.[175] Rabbi Frank noted that the reasoning based on obligation is not necessarily conclusive, but, nevertheless, in this case there is no doubt that ten women can make up the necessary quorum, as the requirement for a minyan here is based on pirsumei nissa, acknowledging the miracle in public.[176] For this purpose, it is agreed that the presence of ten women constitutes the requisite "public." Women meet the requirements of the halakhah by hearing the Megillah in the presence of ten women and therefore recite the berakhah *ha-rav et riveinu* after the reading. (Unlike the berakhot before the reading, the concluding berakhah requires the presence of a minyan.)[177]

Under certain circumstances the Megillah may be read before the normal date, and at such times a minyan is required.[178] In Jerusalem, if the fifteenth of Adar falls on Shabbat, the Megillah is read on the fourteenth, raising the question of whether such a reading is considered "before the normal date." Rabbi Yehudah Eliezer Waldenberg, following the same reasoning as Rabbi Frank (and noting the approval of Rabbi Haim Zonenfeld), similarly rules that in such years "it is clear and obvious as a matter of *din* that ten women can gather *lekhateḥilah* to hear the reading of the Megillah and recite all the berakhot."[179] Rema's doubt, he explains, was whether men and women may join together to form a minyan.[180] But there is no doubt about women alone forming a minyan for the Megillah reading.

Thus, concludes Rabbi Ovadiah Yosef,

> we reject that which R. Menasheh Klein wrote in *Mishneh Halakhot* against the custom of women to make a minyan for themselves to read the Megillah. His arguments are not clear.

> On the contrary, we should encourage such activities, provided the reader is an expert able to read correctly.[181]

Women's Prayer Groups

Evaluating the women's prayer groups that have been established over the last decade or two is a more complicated matter. In an age of egalitarianism, many people surely wonder what would motivate women to set up a single-sex prayer group; and in a period of religious subjectivity and exploration, most people are surprised that such an experiment would need any justification at all. But these groups are meeting the needs of a very select group of women. Seriously educated in Jewish sources and experiences, they want as full participation as possible in communal prayer. In an Orthodox shul, they find that they are excluded from full participation in the service. But because of their commitment to halakhic constraints, they do not wish to pray in a synagogue where men and women sit together and fully participate in all activities, including aliyot to the Torah. Faced with this conflict, some have formed communal women's prayer groups, in which women meet to pray together.

Meeting only infrequently, they maintain their participation in the community's "regular" services. Acknowledging that certain prayers require the presence of a halakhic minyan consisting of ten adult males, the members of the women's groups, when assembled as a group, recite only those prayers that can be said by individuals. One would think that their longings for a deeper religious experience would be welcomed by most halakhists.

Yet these prayer groups—careful not to call themselves minyanim—have met with strident opposition, generated (surprisingly) not from the "right" but from a circle of Talmudists at Yeshiva University's Rabbi Isaac Elchanan Theological Seminary.[182] On what basis could anyone object to these groups? The opposition is clearly sociological, drawing on fears that such prayer groups will undermine traditional positions by granting legitimacy to feminist criticisms of halakhic Judaism. Such concerns are far from unreasonable, but the protest is framed in halakhic terms.

The opposition centers on three main points. First, it is argued that women are actually required to hear the public reading of the Torah and participate in a minyan. This, however, requires a very forced reading of the texts and goes against centuries of normative halakhic practice. Halakhah recognizes that men and women have different obligations in many areas of life. Thus, while men and women are required to pray daily, women are exempt from any obligation to pray with a minyan. They therefore are free to excuse themselves from the general congregation and pray separately without a minyan or a public Torah reading.

Second, there have been ad hominem attacks on the organizers of women's prayer groups. Irrespective of the theoretically benign quality of the women's prayer service, it is said, the organizers are "feminists" who aim at undermining and attacking fundamental halakhic norms and values. But, as has eventually been conceded, the motivation of these women stems from a desire to remain *within* the halakhic system. Pushed on by their rich Jewish backgrounds, they are careful to explore their religious needs within halakhic constraints.

Third, the women's prayer groups use a sefer Torah for a public reading. This, to be sure, is a radical departure from tradition, where women not only did not receive aliyot, but in many cases refrained from even touching a Torah scroll.

The details of the debate over women's prayer groups are not our major concern here. Rabbi Avraham Weiss, one of the main supporters of the groups, has addressed the major issues in his sensitive and effective defense, *Women at Prayer.*[183] Regarding the third objection, R. Weiss devotes a chapter to "Women and Sefer Torah," concluding:

> Prayer is a moment of deep relationship between the human being and God. For many, that moment is more deeply expressed when carrying, holding, touching, kissing the deepest reflection of God's love—the Torah. The right of women to experience this moment—indeed, their right to have contact with the *Sefer Torah*—has a clear basis in the halakhah.[184]

As for reading from the Torah, R. Weiss argues that there is no objection to women reading the Torah in a private capacity, and the prayer groups are not conducting a halakhic public reading, as is underlined by the fact that they do not say Barekhu before reading from the Torah. Such a reading does not have the same raison d'etre—fulfilling a halakhic obligation—as a regular reading in a minyan. But R. Weiss closes his presentation with a quotation from Rabbi J. David Bleich, an outspoken opponent of these groups. R. Bleich originally opposed the public menorahs set up on Ḥanukkah by Lubavitch, arguing that they "serve no halakhic function, either obligatory or discretionary." But he came to accept them because of the positive impact they had on the many Jews who saw them. "I need not explain, or even understand, that phenomenon. It is sufficient to say that it is real and it is salutary." Noting the real and salutary effects on the participants, R. Weiss calls for a similar attitude toward women's prayer groups and their Torah readings.

Why then have these groups not become more popular, especially when R. Weiss quotes the opinion of the late Rabbi Moshe Feinstein, Torah master of our generation, who summarily rejects all theoretical arguments against them. Reb Moshe opined that

> . . . if there is a group of righteous women whose intention is for the sake of Heaven without intending to undermine God's Torah or Jewish practice, then, of course, why prevent them from praying together?
>
> And they may also read from the Torah Scroll, provided that they take care not to do it in such a way that one might erroneously believe it to be a public reading.[185]

I believe that there are three main reasons for the relatively slow growth of these groups. First, many Orthodox women are quite satisfied with their rather passive role in public communal prayer. Just as most men are happy not to act as ḥazzan and are not resentful that they cannot offer the priestly blessing, so most women are not upset that they cannot lead the service or get an aliyah. But, of course, this does not bother participants in women's prayer groups. They are not asking that these groups be universally accepted, only that they be accepted for those women who would grow religiously from participating.

Second, unstated by all concerned, is, I think, a perception that women's prayer groups are a challenge to the individual synagogue rabbi rather than the halakhic system. The meḥitzah in the main synagogue is not offensive to the women who participate in these groups; if it were, they could simply go to a Conservative synagogue. It is, as we noted above, the *absence* of the meḥitzah at the daily minyan that is offensive, the tacit assumption that women would not—or should not—want to attend. There is little attempt on the part of many pulpit rabbis to encourage women to participate in services to the full extent allowed (or demanded) by halakhah; women's prayer groups are no exception. Indeed, there is often an unstated subtle attempt at discouragement. Moreover, to encourage these groups would be interpreted by some, I fear, as an admission that something is wrong in the regular synagogue. Hence the somewhat disingenuous arguments against women's groups.

But it is the third factor—for the most part unaddressed by R. Weiss—that is the most troubling. In general society, imitation may be the highest form of flattery. But in religious society, mimicry has the quality of ersatz mitzvah. Non-Orthodox groups regularly create new berakhot or "reassign" traditional berakhot to new occasions. But from a halakhic perspective, reciting such berakhot constitutes a serious religious offense and is not a positive religious expression.

The argument surrounding a berakhah said during the aliyot at women's prayer services exposes the difficulty. At a halakhic public reading of the Torah, the oleh first recites Barekhu, then repeats the congregational response. This is followed by a berakhah *asher baḥar banu,* the Torah reading, and a concluding berakhah *asher natan lanu*. Barekhu requires a minyan, so it is omitted at Torah readings at women's services. The concluding berakhah, argues Rabbi Saul Berman, may be said after a private reading;[186] hence some groups include it. But all authorities agree that the opening berakhah may only be said before a halakhic public reading.

Yet many of the prayer groups include this first berakhah. Their reasoning is as follows. There is an identical personal blessing which must be said once each day, before one engages in Torah study. If an individual neglects to say the berakhah in the morning, the obligation is fulfilled by saying the Ahavah Rabbah paragraph before Keriat Shema, the content of which is very similar. If an olah deliberately omits saying the berakhah in the morning, refrains from Torah study until the Torah scroll is taken out, and intentionally excludes herself from the exemption obtained through saying the Ahavah Rabbah paragraph, then, the argument goes, she can say the private blessing before her Torah reading so that it looks like the berakhah said at a public reading.

Using a Torah comes naturally. But saying this berakhah under such circumstances comes across as artificial and forced, if only for the fact that the woman, having not said the private *birkhat ha-Torah,* must refrain from any discussion of Torah all morning until she gets her aliyah (and probably must avoid hearing the aliyot that precede hers).

This pattern of imitation, clearly in opposition to Reb Moshe's caution, is defended by R. Weiss, even though he notes that the Rav, Rabbi Joseph B. Soloveitchik, specifically objected to this type of berakhah arrangement. R. Weiss correctly takes to task those who quote this very specific and limited objection to portray the Rav as opposed to women's prayer groups in general when in fact he encouraged their formation. Nonetheless, he ignores the criticism of one of his most important supporters, arguing only its technical points.

This approach is evident to those familiar with women's services. For example, in a regular public reading, Kaddish is said after the seventh aliyah to indicate that the required reading has been completed. The person who will read the Haftarah is called, and the maftir is repeated from the Torah reading so as not to "shame" the person who is called to read from the prophets as opposed to the Torah. Kaddish requires a minyan, so it is omitted by women's groups. Then, despite the fact that the participants clearly claim that theirs is not the required Torah reading, the maftir is repeated with no reason other than to mimic the regular reading. It would be more logical to have the person who reads the last section continue with the Haftarah (as is regularly done, for example, at the Minḥah reading on Yom Kippur).

The problem, in a way, is not that women's groups have gone too far, but that they have not gone far enough. There has been little attempt to make use of the license granted by the lack of a minyan to create new approaches. R. Berman reported in a lecture at the Lincoln Square Synagogue that the Rav had suggested to him that inasmuch as the repetition of the Amidah (and *Kedushah*) must be excluded in the absence of a minyan, the *Kedushah* of U-va le-Tziyyon (which requires no minyan) should be added after the silent Amidah. Here is creative counsel that draws on traditional motifs and adapts them for a new context. But in most women's prayer groups, the ḥazzan it simply stands silent while the other participants say the private Amidah and then says her own silent Amidah aloud to mimic the regular repetition.

In a sense, R. Weiss's *Women at Prayer* has provided an opportunity to take a more creative approach to women's prayer groups. Under siege by a series of disingenuous halakhic criticisms, the organizers of these groups and their advisors have often misinterpreted critiques of specific forms as part of the general campaign against them. This is not an atmosphere for reconsideration of approaches and appropriate experimentation. Now that the technical halakhic permissibility of women's prayer groups is on the record for all to see, the time may be right for a calmer discussion between congregational rabbis and those in their synagogues who would find such prayer groups religiously enhancing.

New forms have to emerge organically from the group members trying out new motifs as they live their experiment. We present here a few thoughts on the Torah reading by way of offering a model for approaching the issue. The key problem is to distinguish between mimicry and authenticity.

It might help to consider an imagined proposal for an all-male minyan. Let us suppose that a group of men in a shul resents the fact that only some congregants, by virtue of an accident of birth, can ascend the *dukhan* to bless the congregation during the repetition of the holiday Amidah. These privileged few, Kohanim all, have no special qualifications, certainly no spiritual superiority over the more learned and pious members of the congregation. The non-Kohanim therefore make the following arrangement.

They form a special minyan, asking the Kohanim to pray with the regular minyan. A very carefully chosen group of pious men is selected to bless the worshippers in the new minyan. Levites wash their hands—certainly there is nothing wrong with that—and after Modim they ascend the *dukhan,* put their tallitot over their heads, extend their hands (being careful to not do so in the traditional manner peculiar to Kohanim), and mutter a short prayer when the ḥazzan pauses on cue: "We hope You will allow to bless Your people with love." They say it softly, raising their voices only for the last word (*be-ahavah*). The congregants, prompted to the fact that this is not a real berakhah, do not answer amen.

Then, as the ḥazzan recites the traditional paragraph said when Kohanim are not present, these would-be Kohanim repeat each word of the priestly blessing aloud. (After all, they are only reciting verses of the Torah.) Again, the congregation answers Ken yehi ratzon instead of amen.

On what basis could one object to this? Certainly the technical argument that everyone is required to be silent during the repetition of the Amidah misses the point. So does the protest that most people see no need for such a service—they are not the ones advocating its establishment. Yet I think that everyone reading this description senses the unauthentic mimicry, a charge we would not make when a non-Kohen uses the very same verses in blessing his children on Friday nights.

Of course, the parallelism is hardly airtight. Kohanim are set aside by the Torah as those designated to bless the congregation with certain verses. Women are excluded from aliyot nowadays for "social" reasons, not because they were excluded by the original halakhah. A parent using the same verses on Friday night is not pretending to be a Kohen, but is simply transferring the power and symbolism of the verses to another situation.

Even though the women's reading is not the halakhically required public Torah reading, it undoubtedly is authentic to read the regular parashah, the focal point for many a Shabbat discussion. And it is understandable that a sefer Torah would be used. The sefer has the power to inspire and uplift;[187] that is why we dance with it on Simḥat Torah even though there is no halakhic reason for doing so. It also is appropriate to have a number of aliyot, since part of the reason for the reading is to offer different people the opportunity for intimate contact with the sefer Torah. But the idea of seven aliyot is part of the definition of the halakhic reading; the segments indicated in the Ḥumash and the standard number called up should be seen as nothing more than a convenient division of the text to be adjusted as necessary for the women's group. There is no logic (other than mimicry) to repeating a Torah section for the maftir, as indicated above. The person receiving the last aliyah should read the maftir.

Certainly there is no justification for restricting the first aliyah to a *bat Kohen.* The daughter of a Kohen loses such priestly rights as being able to eat terumah when she marries, and a bat Yisrael gains such rights upon marrying a Kohen; there is no reason to honor a *bat Kohen* with the first aliyah. Even the Halakhah Committee of the (Conservative) Rabbinical Assembly of Israel, which follows the non-Orthodox custom of giving women aliyot in regular services, argues against such a policy:

> [The] first aliya is not just a fringe benefit but rather one of the main rituals that a Kohen does and thus by allowing women to fulfill this function the people will think that a woman can be a Kohen, an idea that has no basis in Jewish tradition. . . . [In Conservative] congregations where women

receive aliyot, a *bat Kohen* and a *bat Levi* have the same status as an Israelite.[188]

There is no disagreement that Barekhu requires a minyan and must be omitted at a women's prayer group. Whether or not to recite the second berakhah rests on a halakhic debate concerning the necessity of a minyan, a common occurrence in halakhah. One simply follows the decision of the group's halakhic advisor.

It is the opening berakhah that is problematic, as we indicated earlier. This is not only because of its forced and manipulative nature, as if not studying Torah all morning (because the private berakhah has not been said) were an appropriate way to prepare for an aliyah. It also feeds into the popular misconception that it is the berakhah that establishes the religious integrity of the action. Indeed, originally only the first person receiving an aliyah recited the opening berakhah and only the last person recited the closing one. However, since worshippers who arrived after the beginning of the Torah reading or departed before its conclusion would miss one berakhah or the other, it was decided to have both berakhot said for each aliyah.

Originally, when women too received aliyot, they—like most of the men—did not say *birkhot ha-Torah*. But they apparently did say Barekhu. "It was only *birkhot ha-Torah* that were originally not said; Barekhu was recited," writes Ḥatam Sofer.[189] And there is an authentic motif related to Barekhu that can be easily adapted to women's prayer groups: the zimmun. Both Barekhu and zimmun constitute a call to the public to praise God, coupled with a public response. Barekhu, which in effect calls upon the congregation to focus on the Torah reading, requires a minyan; but, as we have already discussed, zimmun is fully legitimate in an all-female community. Zimmun is, in a sense, the analog to Barekhu in a women's group.

The Talmud suggests two source texts for the zimmun: "Exalt the Lord with me; let us extol His name together" (Psalms 34:4), and "For the name of the Lord I proclaim; give glory to our God" (Deuteronomy 32:3).[190] It would, I think, capture and adapt the original dynamics for the olah to call out one of the verses and have the congregation respond with the other (or some variant, such as her calling out half of one verse, the congregation completing it, and her then reciting the second). This is how, I believe, one begins to create authentic novel forms for a legitimate new experience.

The jury is still out on the fate of women's prayer groups. If synagogues become more sensitive to women's needs and the prayer groups stagnate in their current pattern, they will probably not grow past their present status. If their organizers reach out, interact with allies in the broader halakhic community, and draw on a wider circle of participants, they may yet add a totally new and exciting dimension to our religious community. As R. Berman points out,

> . . . we must encourage women to develop in a creative fashion whatever additional forms they find necessary for their religious growth. I would not presume to know what new religious developments could emerge from Jewish women consciously setting for themselves the task of discovering customs expressive of their religious feelings in contemporary society. Their practices might involve their own form of public worship to follow and supplement the standard service, but expressive of women's sensitivities. It might involve the creation of new religious artifacts or of new patterns of communal study. Only one thing is certain, and that is that the

creative religious energies of Jewish women remain a major source of untapped strength for the Jewish community as a whole, and those energies must be freed.[191]

In Our Schools

Yeshiva Education for Women

The late Rebbetzin Tonya Soloveitchik once struck up a conversation with a little girl from Williamsburg and asked her whether she attended Bais Yaakov. "Bais Yaakov?!" stammered the girl in wide-eyed horror. "Dort—dort—dort lernt men khimesh! [There . . . there . . . there . . . they learn Ḥumash!]."[192] We understand her uneasiness, of course. The Satmar Rebbe felt that women should engage in only the most superficial textual study of Torah.[193] Perish the thought that any of his followers attend a school whose educational policy contradicts the Rebbe's teachings.

The Satmar Rebbe's position may not resonate well within the Modern Orthodox community, but all must concede that distinctiveness of obligation applies within halakhah to the issue of learning Torah too. All Jews, men and women, have an obligation to live a Torah life; study of Torah is a logical prerequisite to actualizing Torah in one's life. But there is another dimension of

Talmud Torah, study for its own sake as a purely intellectual endeavor, which is not obligatory for women.

Of course, halakhic exemption does not usually mean exclusion. And, indeed, there is little reason for a woman to want to exclude herself from Talmud Torah. "Intellectual redemption through the study of Torah resembles, in its structure, the redemption through prayer," notes the Rav. "It was for a good reason that Moses and Ezra integrated keriat haTorah into the framework of tefila. Without Talmud Torah it would be difficult for tefila to assure man of total redemption."[194]

There is a long-standing halakhic debate over the extent to which women's exemption from some aspects of Talmud Torah includes a prohibition of studying specific sections of the Oral Law. The face rulings in Rambam and Shulḥan Arukh may seem to argue against allowing it, but the details of this halakhic debate are not our major concern here.

A century ago it was revolutionary to suggest that women should have a serious grounding in, say, Ḥumash, Rashi, and the other traditional commentaries. The Bais Yaakov curriculum, taken for granted today throughout most of the "yeshiva world," has no precedent in former generations of Torah education. It is now regarded as the Torah norm in many circles, despite the fact that it did not arise organically from traditional attitudes but rather as a response to the specific needs of Jewish women in general society. And it was introduced without any learned discussion of the halakhic sources.

> It appears to me [wrote Ḥafetz Ḥayyim] that this [prohibition against women learning Torah] applies only to past times. . . . Nowadays, as parental tradition has been weakened and we find young women who in general do not live close

> to home and in particular regularly study secular subjects, it is certainly a mitzvah to teach them Bible and rabbinic ethics [*musar*]. . . . Otherwise they may stray from God's path.[195]

It was not the text of Shulḥan Arukh that was the source of the decision to expand the bounds of Torah education for women; it was the sociological reality and strategies for confronting it. Nowadays, the *be-di'avad* position regarding advanced Jewish education for women has become the *lekhateḥilah* normative attitude for the bulk of the Orthodox community.

Of course, there is a wide spectrum of opinion among halakhists regarding Torah education for women, with the view of the Satmar Rebbe at one end and that of the Rav, Rabbi Joseph B. Soloveitchik, on the other. (In setting up his Maimonides Yeshiva in Brookline, Massachusetts, the Rav deliberately provided equal opportunity in Torah studies for boys and girls;[196] and when the Anglo-Jewish press carried a photo of his inaugural shiur at the Stern College Beit Medrash, there was little doubt that he felt serious Talmud study had a significant, legitimate place in a woman's Torah education.)

Unfortunately, there is a (not so) subtle campaign in some circles to avoid presenting women's study of the Oral Law as a normative halakhic practice. Thus, for example, Rabbi Jacob J. Schacter notes that the ArtScroll translation of Rabbi Barukh Halevi Epstein's *Mekor Barukh* (published as *My Uncle the Netziv*) skips over very significant words that might be unsettling. In describing the learned first wife of the Netziv, for instance, R. Epstein wrote:

> It was her habit to sit by the oven in the kitchen—even in the summertime—next to a table piled high with *seforim*.

> These included a *Tanach,* [*Mishnayot,*] *Ein Yaacov,* various *midrashim,* . . . and many other books of this type [and *Sifrei Aggadah*]. Much of her time and attention were dedicated to poring over these books, which interested her far more than running a household.[197]

The words in brackets, which show his aunt's involvement in studying the Oral Law, appear in the original Hebrew but were left out in the ArtScroll translation.

Such misrepresentations, whether subtle or blatant, have an impact even in the Modern Orthodox community. But given the Rav's enthusiastic endorsement of women learning Talmud, we wonder why not all of our yeshivot include formal Talmud classes for women. Some years ago, a coed elementary yeshiva that separates boys and girls in the upper grades instituted accelerated ninth-year math for all boy eighth graders but kept regular eighth-grade math for the girl eighth graders. (After all, "everyone knows" that boys are better than girls in math.) Needless to say, the parents would not stand for such educational nonsense; soon there were advanced classes for the better students—male and female—and regular classes for the average students. It made no sense to automatically exclude girls from an advanced math class. Why, then, is there little vigorous protest when the girls are denied Talmud?

The situation is all the more unintelligible when we realize that most yeshivot offer young women shiurim in subjects that clearly are within the Oral Law and outside the curriculum suggested by Ḥafetz Ḥayyim. When we teach Vayikra, notes Rabbi Aharon Lichtenstein, we certainly include Rashi,

> and Rashi cites sources from *Torah She'b'al Peh.* It is impossible to decide to teach women Rashi but not *Mishna* when Rashi

> himself cites *Mishnayot.* The fact that a particular *Mishna* filters down to a woman via her studying Rashi does not change its status of being a *Mishna.* It is impossible to teach "at the tip of a fork." Either the material is to be studied or it's not to be studied.[198]

We expect all our students to know the basics of a halakhic life-style and to ask their *posek* when they do not know the answer to a complicated question. But it would never occur to any serious yeshiva educator to simply give boys lists of halakhot without the training to enable them to look up something in Mishnah Berurah before asking a question. How, then, is it possible for girls to graduate without the proficiency to deal with a Mishnah Berurah? Certainly we would not want to have teachers—male or female—who could not consult basic sources themselves and could be counted on only to hand out lists that they had either copied when in school or been handed by someone else.

The reason that Talmud is sometimes excluded from the girls' course of study cannot be that they do not go on to advanced Talmud study; this argument would have terminated yeshiva elementary schools for girls before their high schools were organized. The claim that women are not interested in going to Talmud shiurim as adults only shows that people will not pursue advanced studies if they are first not given the basics and then are discouraged from advancing. As Devora Steinmetz of the Drisha Institute and Beit Rabban points out,

> Too many voices call out against women's learning [Talmud], many in our own communities. Opportunities for learned women to share their learning are too limited. For those women who do learn, the future is uncertain. And, still, too many allow their dreams to die, because they are afraid to

> pursue the course of their dreams only to find that, further down the road, the doors are still closed to them.[199]

Boys are taught Talmud in Modern Orthodox yeshivot not only in the hope that they will go on to become *talmidei ḥakhamim,* but because a true understanding of Torah and halakhah is closed to someone who cannot open a Talmud or a sefer halakhah. In our system of education, elementary and high schools teach all the basic skills to everyone. In our society, serious exposure to Talmud is a required basic skill, and girls as well as boys should master it. "To my mind," wrote R. Lichtenstein,

> it is desirable and necessary, not only possible, to provide intensive education for women from *Torah Shebe-al Pe* sources, whether resorting to the argument that since women are engaged in all professions, why should they be specifically limited regarding Torah, or because of the words of the Chofetz Chaim (when Beit Yaakov was founded) that if the Rambam can say that it is necessary to teach a convert the essentials of Judaism, an individual who grows up in a Jewish context should all the more so be afforded such an education.[200]

The Lubavitcher Rebbe, Rabbi Menaḥem Mendel Schneersohn, expresses a similarly positive attitude when he says that under current societal conditions, "not only is it *permitted* to teach [women] the Oral Torah, but, more than that, one *must* teach it to them."[201] He remarks that throughout the generations, when women were taught at home, many of them—not just a select few—were proficient in the Oral Torah. Nowadays, it is not only the increased general educational opportunities for women that motivate teaching them the Oral Torah. Mothers are expected to help and encourage their children with their Torah studies, and this requires them to be literate in what their sons learn, which includes Mishnah and the rest of the Oral Torah.

The reluctance to offer formal Talmud classes for girls is all the more inconsistent with our needs and general educational attitudes when we realize that yeshivot offer not only Rashi, but, as R. Lichtenstein noted, Mishnah and Torah she-be-al peh courses in which the page of Talmud is studied from a source book rather than a standard Gemara. Clearly we are dealing with social mores rather than halakhah. When a girl who learns Mishnah responds to a suggestion that she attends a particular yeshiva with the shocked protest that "There . . . there . . . there the girls learn Talmud!" she is reflecting a social allegiance, not a halakhic commitment. As David Bernstein commented,

> Even where actual Talmud study is not called "Talmud," it is called *Torah shebe-al pe* or Mishna, and the pages of Talmud are studied from xeroxed sheets. The difference is purely semantic; the words of Rav and Shmuel, whether in a bound *masekhet* from the Va'ad haYeshivot or on a xeroxed page, are the same words. Clearly, there is no longer a halakhic argument in these cases, rather a political one.[202]

There may be some hesitation among young women to undertake formal Talmud study, not simply because societal support is often missing, but because the first step in learning Talmud is often difficult and tedious, and there are few public role-models. They need encouragement from our community, not self-fulfilling assessments that there is no point in such study. In a way, it is comparable to the situation of math education for young women in the general society. We should approach Talmud illiteracy with at least the same vigor that our general society—and our Modern Orthodox yeshivot—approach math illiteracy.

"Halakha does differentiate between men and women in this matter [of learning Torah], and their respective life roles are also different. But when one speaks about the ability to study a page of Talmud, to understand and enjoy it, I see no reason to deny these teachings to women," wrote R. Lichtenstein, suggesting,

> It is appropriate to teach the *Sedarim* of *Zeraim, Moed,* and *Nezikin* and the small amount of applicable material in *Nashim, Kodashim* and *Taharot*. And when these areas are taught, they must be taught in depth. It is even necessary to establish this as an integral part of the school curriculum, an actual *shiur*. This is the way I teach my daughter and so was my wife educated. This seems to me to be the recommended approach regarding the women of our generation.[203]

If a principal asserts that "girls don't really need Talmud, so why make a fuss about it not being offered," parents should respond as vigorously as they would if he or she was unwilling to offer more than the minimum state requirement in math to female students.

Women Rabbis

The issue of women's ordination is not a pressing one in the Modern Orthodox community—and the reason is simple. From a practical perspective, most professional positions previously restricted to rabbis are now open to women. Jewish educational institutions are regularly headed and staffed by women, despite the fact that they lack a rabbinical title.[204] They set educational agendas and increasingly wield real power in our educational system.

Interestingly, the stationery of some schools now lists

the title "Rebb" (for Rebbetzin) before the names of female administrators. It makes no sense to suggest either that a principal merits specific authority simply by virtue of her husband's *semikhah* (rabbinic ordination) or that she would be less impressive an administrator if her husband was, say, a well-learned lawyer or businessman who had not completed a formal *semikhah* program. The fact that a good number of female educational administrators are in fact married to rabbis has allowed for a temporary solution to the anomalous situation whereby individuals have attained professional stature for which an appropriate title is not yet available. In some schools, the principal's or teacher's own earned doctorate allows for a better and more obvious solution.

In Israel, women are now admitted as "pleaders" in rabbinic courts. They function as lawyers, representing clients and arguing cases before the battei din that have official standing in Israel in matters of marriage, divorce, and family status. This developed as an offshoot of a practice originally devised for men. In order to make it possible for rabbis who were not lawyers (but were obviously qualified to argue cases) to appear before the courts, men who had extensive yeshiva training were admitted as pleaders. All lawyers who are members of the bar have standing to appear before all Israeli state courts; hence nonreligious female lawyers could appear before rabbinic courts. Since it then made no sense to disqualify trained female religious pleaders, they were granted status. This is a pattern that we shall see repeated in many areas of rabbinic life.

Semikhah generally requires some mastery of talmudic and halakhic sources and a test on basic issues, usually centered around kashrut. But standards differ drastically from one institution or individual to another, and the degree in and of itself is not always testimony to true mastery. Hence, having earned *semikhah* from some yeshiva or individual does not automatically guarantee respect in the Orthodox community, and a knowledgeable "layman" who is known to "sit and learn" will constantly be asked his opinion, both on academic and practical halakhic matters. Thus, as the current Chief Rabbi of Israel wrote, "women may be gedolei ha-dor . . . [and] serve as *morei hora'ah* [*posekot*] and teachers of Torah and practical halakhah, as the authority for these positions flows from the individual's talents."[205]

If I were to hazard a guess, I would say that one of the areas of halakhah that will first attract women will be *niddah,* not kashrut. As women become more learned, they will want to ask their own *she'elot,* and considerations of *tzeniut* will make them gravitate toward women decisors (*posekot*). As Chana Henkin of Nishmat noted, "Women qualified to answer *niddah* questions would certainly make a significant contribution to Torah observance today, and we should work to qualify such women."[206] In this respect, the question of women rabbis will be settled not in the admissions offices of rabbinical schools, but in the journals publishing Torah and halakhah articles written by women. We should not expect any great halakhic change to result from the appearance of such *posekot,* however. Halakhic decisors are interpreting Torat Hashem, not imposing a male view on God's Torah.[207]

In any event, women have already gained professional entry into the world of the Orthodox rabbi. They teach and function as administrators in yeshivot; they lecture and hold prominent positions in Jewish public life; their counsel is sought by those who know and respect their knowledge. It is, however, clear that they will be denied the privilege of preaching from the pulpit during services. Halakhah demands separation during services. While a woman's occupancy of the pulpit would have symbolic importance, the fact is that the pulpit is no longer the exclusive center of power that it once was.[208] From a practical point of view, it is much more important for women to have access to the podium at synagogue or yeshiva shiurim than to the pulpit.

Recently, I overheard a young high school rebbe casually remark to his shiur that when he had gone through the sugya at home with his wife, she had proposed an alternative and more correct way of understanding the discussion. No one in the class reacted as if he had said anything out of the ordinary. When this becomes more commonplace—and when the wives themselves start giving the shiurim in our schools—our whole discussion will take on a different face.

Of course, human nature is such that accomplished people generally desire some sort of formal recognition. Moreover, simple tax considerations (like parsonage, which is available only to clergy) may force the creation of a formal title as more women become professionals taking on roles normally associated with rabbis. But given the fact that the ordination of women was initiated outside the halakhic community, social reality dictates that there will be learned Modern Orthodox women acting as non-pulpit rabbis long before they have the formal title.

Conclusion

Many people still oppose increased women's participation in ritual and communal religious life. They see things only in terms of resisting feminism and fighting egalitarianism, searching for leaders who are misleading religious women to blame for the new issues that are being raised, targets that can be identified in the fight to maintain old perspectives. This attitude is worse than fruitless. As Joseph C. Kaplan has pointed out,

> . . . the impetus propelling the changes in the traditional women's role in Judaism does not flow from a charismatic and dynamic leadership. Rather, it is an expression of the *vox populi,* emanating from the rank and file of those women and men who seek more equality, more responsibility, and more involvement within and with a commitment to the halakhic process. From these same grass roots has arisen the ceremony of *Simhat Bat* celebrating the birth of a daughter, a Torah-oriented rather than party-oriented *Bat Mitsva,* and women's Torah study groups, yeshivot and prayer services. Such a

> movement, a movement from within, with all its problems, has a certain innate strength and conviction that bodes well for the ultimate success of its admirable goals.[209]

We must come to terms with this new reality. We can ignore or fight it at our own risk, or acknowledge the new possibilities for growth in Torah that it offers. As David Berger observes,

> Needless to say, the Torah does envision different religious roles and obligations for men and women, and no amount of apologetics can or should wholly erase those distinctions. The argument that even permissible actions should sometimes be restricted because of the direction in which they lead is by no means frivolous. At the same time, permissible expressions of piety and a thirst for the word of God deserve our utmost respect, not only with regard to women's issues but along the entire spectrum of concerns that divide, challenge, and stimulate the Orthodox community.[210]

Our own personal religious integrity—and that of our leaders—will be judged by our response to this challenge. There will be a price to pay if religious women, trained in their everyday lives to think of themselves as full participants in the process of becoming complete persons, come to the conclusion that they have not been taken seriously by their religious and educational leaders.

Glossary

Words set in SMALL CAPITALS are defined elsewhere in the Glossary.

Al ha-Nissim. Extra paragraph added to AMIDAH and BIRKHAT HA-MAZON on Ḥanukkah and Purim.

Aliyah (pl. **aliyot**). Honor of "going up" to the Torah when it is read during the synagogue service.

Amidah. Main prayer of morning, afternoon, and evening services; recited while standing.

Asher bara. Last of the SHEVA BERAKHOT.

Ashkenazic. Of or pertaining to Jews and Jewish culture of Central and Eastern European origin.

Ba'al [masc.], **Ba'alat** [fem.] **ha-bayit.** Head of the household.

Bar mitzvah (pl. **benei mitzvah**). Thirteen-year-old boy; the age of majority.

Bat mitzvah (pl. **benot mitzvah**). Twelve-year-old girl; the age of majority.

Be-di'avad. Post facto acceptance of less-than-optimal situation.

Bet midrash. House of study. Also, common designation of smaller "chapel" of synagogue, where daily services are held.

Berakhah (pl. **berakhot**). Liturgical blessing, usually beginning with "Blessed are You, Hashem, King of the universe."

Berit milah. Ritual circumcision.

Birkhat ha-gomel. BERAKHAH said in public after surviving potentially dangerous situation.

Birkhat ha-mazon. BERAKHOT said after meal, sometimes referred to as grace after meals.

Birkhat ha-zimmun. Prefatory "invitation" to say BIRKHAT HA-MAZON added when proper quorum of three persons have eaten together.

Davar she-bikdushah. Prayer that can be said only in the presence of ten adult men.

Devar Torah (pl. **divrei Torah**). Short discourse on Torah subject.

Dukhan. Raised platform from which KOHANIM deliver priestly blessing. As verb, it means to deliver priestly blessing.

Gedolei Torah. Major authoritative religious authorities.

Gemara. Discussions in TALMUD that explicate the MISHNAH.

Gaon (pl. **geonim**). Major rabbinic intellect.

Haftarah. Reading from the Prophets on Sabbath, festivals and fasts.

Haggadah. Liturgical retelling of Exodus read at Passover SEDER.

Ḥagigah. Celebration.

Halakhah. The system of Jewish law, comprising ritual, economic, and ethical components.

Halakhot. Specific legal details of HALAKHAH.

Ha-motzi. BERAKHAH said before eating bread at opening of meal.

Havdalah. Ceremony marking end of SHABBAT.

Ḥazal. Rabbinic Sages.

Ḥazzan. Cantor who leads synagogue service.

Heter. Lenient halakhic ruling. *See* HALAKHAH.

Ḥumash. Pentateuch.

Ḥumrah. Stringent halakhic ruling. *See* HALAKHAH.

Ḥuppah. Canopy under which marriage ceremony is held.

Kaddish. Mourner's prayer.

Kashrut. Jewish dietary laws.

Kiddush. Ceremony over wine which opens Friday night SHABBAT meal.

Kohen (pl. **Kohanim**). Descendant of Aaron the High Priest.

Kol ishah. A woman's voice.

Leḥem mishneh. Two loaves of bread or challah over which HA-MOTZI is recited at start of SHABBAT meal.

Lekhateḥilah. Preferred opinion or strategy.

Levi (pl. **Levi'im**). Levite; descendant of tribe of LEVI.

Maftir. Selection from HAFTARAH read after Torah reading on SHABBAT and holidays.

Masorah. Tradition.

Megillah. Scroll; usually refers to scroll of Esther, read on Purim.

Meḥitzah. Physical barrier in synagogue separating men's and women's sections.

Mikveh. Ritual bath.

Minhag. Custom.

Minḥah. Afternoon prayer.

Minyan. Quorum of ten adults required for recitation of certain prayers. In general, ten adult men are required.

Mishnah. Section of TALMUD which contains first postbiblical codification of HALAKHAH.

Mitzvah. Religiously praiseworthy and/or required act.

Musaf. Prayer service added after SHAḤARIT on SHABBAT and holidays.

Niddah. Period initiated by menstrual flow during which wife and husband may not have intimate relations.

Nusaḥ. Liturgical tradition.

Oneg Shabbat (pl. **Ongei Shabbat**). Informal Friday night communal gathering.

Posek (pl. **posekim** [masc.], **posekot** [fem.]). Authoritative decisor of halakhic questions. *See* HALAKHAH.

Rebbe. Teacher of TALMUD.

Responsum (pl. **responsa**). Response from authoritative rabbinic authority to halakhic query.

Retzei. Extra paragraph added to AMIDAH and BIRKHAT HA-MAZON on SHABBAT.

Rosh Ḥodesh. Semi-sanctified day commemorating the beginning of the Jewish month.

Seder. Holiday meal eaten on Passover evening.

Sefer halakhah. Book of HALAKHAH.

Sefer Torah. Scroll of Pentateuch, read aloud during services on Mondays, Thursdays, SHABBAT, and holidays.

Semikhah. Rabbinic ordination.

Sephardic. Of or pertaining to Jews and Jewish culture of Spanish, North African, or Middle Eastern origin.

Seudah shelishit. Third meal eaten on SHABBAT afternoon.

Shabbat (pl. **Shabbatot**) Sabbath.

Shaḥarit. Morning prayer service.

Shalom bayit. Peaceful family interaction.

Shiur. Class.

Sheva Berakhot. Seven BERAKHOT recited during marriage ceremony and repeated under various conditions at each meal eaten by bride and groom during first week of marriage.

Shtibl. Small informal synagogue.

Shul. Synagogue.

Siddur (pl. **siddurim**). Prayer book.

Siyyum. Celebration generally marking completion of learning a tractate of MISHNAH or TALMUD.

Tallit (pl. **tallitot**). Prayer shawl usually worn by men during prayer service.

Talmid ḥakham (pl. **talmidei ḥakhamim**). Person well versed in Jewish law.

Talmud. Basic rabbinic text, consisting of MISHNAH and GEMARA.

Tanakh. Hebrew Bible.

Tefillah. Prayer.

Teshuvah (pl. teshuvot). RESPONSUM.

Torah she-be-al peh. Oral Law that complements Written Law of Bible. Basic text of Oral Law is TALMUD, but term extends to subsequent rabbinic texts, including RESPONSA and halakhic compilations.

Tzitzit. Fringes on four corners of TALLIT.

Ya'aleh ve-Yavo. Extra paragraph added to AMIDAH and BIRKHAT HA-MAZON on ROSH ḤODESH.

Zemirot. Liturgical songs sung during SHABBAT meals.

Zimmun. Invitation to say BIRKHAT HA-MAZON; requires quorum of three.

Notes

Introduction

1. Susan Grossman, "Feminism, Midrash and Mikveh," *Conservative Judaism* 44, no. 2 (Winter 1992): 7.

2. R. Ovadiah Yosef, *Yehave Da'at,* vol. 4 (Jerusalem, 5741 [1981]), responsum 15, pp. 75–78, n. **.

3. R. Yeḥiel Yaakov Weinberg, *Seridei Esh,* vol. 2 (Jerusalem: Mosad Harav Kook, 1977), responsum 8, pp. 13–17.

4. Ibid.

5. It is interesting to note in passing that in the sixties and seventies in America, Torah authorities speaking at conventions of Yavneh, the national association of religious Jewish college students, did not take exception to coed zemirot. Such activities are the norm at contemporary programs of Young Israel, NCSY, and Yeshiva University.

6. R. Moshe Feinstein, *Iggerot Mosheh,* Oraḥ Ḥayyim, part 4 (Bene B'rak: Ohel Yosef, 1974), responsum 49, pp. 80f.

7. Pesaḥim 108a.

8. Rashbam, Pesaḥim 108a, s.v. *ishah einah tzerikha ha-seiba.*

9. R. Ḥayyim David Halevi, *Mayim Ḥayyim,* vol. 1 (Tel Aviv, 5751 [1991]), responsum 10, p. 49f.

10. *Kesef Mishneh* to *Mishneh Torah,* Ḥametz u-Matzah 7:8.

11. Pesaḥim 108a.

12. *Shulḥan Arukh,* Oraḥ Ḥayyim 472:4.

13. See, e.g., R. David Auerbach, *Halikhot Beitah* (Jerusalem, 5743 [1983]), 18:23, n. 73.

14. R. Joseph B. Soloveitchik, *The Lonely Man of Faith* (New York: Doubleday, 1992), p. 4. First published in *Tradition* 7, no. 2 (Summer 1965).

15. R. J. David Bleich, "Women on Synagogue Boards," *Tradition* 15, no. 4 (Spring 1976): 65. He also points out that some go beyond this position, arguing that women are not precluded from being members of legislative or parliamentary bodies, since members of such bodies cannot enforce the laws they enact.

16. Bava Kamma 38a.

17. R. Emanuel Rackman, "Arrogance or Humility in Prayer," *Tradition* 1, no. 1 (Fall 1958): 17. This theme is adopted in R. Norman Lamm's *A Hedge of Roses* (New York: Feldheim, 1987), pp. 75f.

18. R. Saul Berman, "The Status of Women in Halakhic Judaism," *Tradition* 14, no. 2 (Fall 1973): 17.

19. The development of women's responsibility to hear the blowing of the shofar is discussed in Arlene Pianko, "Women and the Shofar," *Tradition* 14, no. 4 (Fall 1974): 53–62.

20. R. Yeḥiel Yaakov Weinberg, *Seridei Esh,* vol. 3, (Jerusalem: Mosad Harav Kook, 1977), responsum 105, p. 322.

21. Esther Krauss, "Communications," *Tradition* 27, no. 2 (Winter 1993): 82.

22. R. Soloveitchik, *Lonely Man of Faith,* pp. 19f.

23. R. Joseph B. Soloveitchik, "Majesty and Humility," *Tradition* 17, no. 2 (Spring 1978), p. 25.

24. R. Joseph B. Soloveitchik, "A Tribute to the Rebbitzen of Telne," *Tradition* 17, no. 2 (Spring 1978), p. 76.

25. Ibid., p. 77.

In Our Homes

26. R. Ḥayyim David Halevi, *Aseh Lekha Rav,* vol. 6 (Tel Aviv: 5745 [1985]), responsum 37, p. 127.

27. Ibid., p. 126.

28. R. Ḥayyim David Halevi, *Aseh Lekha Rav,* vol. 8 (Tel Aviv: 5748 [1988]), responsum 20, p. 47.

29. R. Moshe Feinstein, *Iggerot Mosheh,* Even ha-Ezer, part 2 (New York: Moriah, 5724 [1954]), responsum 12, p. 425.

30. R. Halevi, *Aseh Lekha Rav,* (Tel Aviv: 5741 [1981]), vol. 4, responsum 59, pp. 288f.

31. Ibid., vol. 6, responsum 37, p. 122.

32. *Shulḥan Arukh,* Yoreh De'ah 240:17.

33. R. David Yosef Mescheloff, "Ha-ishah ha-yehudit be-halakhah," *Dinei Yisrael* 13–14 (5746–48 [1986–88]): 263–312. This article includes a serious critique of R. Moshe Meiselman, *Jewish Women in Jewish Law* (New York: Ktav, 1978).

34. Ibid., p. 277.

35. Rambam, *Mishneh Torah,* Hilkhot Yom Tov 6:16–18.

36. Ibid.

37. Avot 2:2.

38. Ḥullin 105b.

39. Tosafot to Berakhot 53b, s.v. *ve-heyitem kedoshim; Tur Shulḥan Arukh,* Oraḥ Ḥayyim 191; *Shulḥan Arukh,* Oraḥ Ḥayyim 181:10.

40. Berakhot 53b; *Tur Shulḥan Arukh,* Oraḥ Ḥayyim 181.

41. R. Moshe Sternbach, *Teshuvot ve-Hanagot* (Jerusalem, 5746 [1986]), responsum 174, p. 61.

42. R. Moshe Eisemann, "Communications," *Tradition* 27, no. 2 (Winter 1993), p. 91.

43. "Monitoring the Media," *Coalition* 10, no. 3 (March 1995), p. 8.

44. *Sefer ha-Yashar—Responsa of Rabbenu Tam,* sec. 70d.

45. Ibid.

46. Ramban to Shabbat 117b.

47. Berakhot 7:1, 45a.

48. Arakhin 3a.

49. Berakhot 45b, s.v. *sha-ani.*

50. Ibid.

51. *Tur Shulḥan Arukh,* Oraḥ Ḥayyim 199.

52. Ibid., s.v. *she-yesh mefarshim le-kayem.*

53. *Tur Shulḥan Arukh,* Oraḥ Ḥayyim 199.

54. *Shulḥan Arukh,* Oraḥ Ḥayyim 199:7.

55. Ibid., Be'urei ha-Gra. This was anticipated by *Sefer ha-Roke'aḥ,* no. 333.

56. Parashat Koraḥ, par. 13.

57. *Mishnah Berurah* to *Shulḥan Arukh,* Oraḥ Ḥayyim 199, n. 16.

58. Berakhot 45b, s.v. *sha-ani.*

59. *Shulḥan Arukh,* Oraḥ Ḥayyim 199:7.

60. E.g., R. David Auerbach, *Halikhot Beitah* (Jerusalem, 5743 [1983]), 12:6, pp. 93ff.; R. Yitzhak Yaakov Fuchs, *Halikhot Bat Yisrael* (Jerusalem, 1983), 3:14, p. 62.

61. Quoted in R. Auerbach, *Halikhot Beitah,* p. 94, n. 14.

62. *Shulḥan Arukh,* Oraḥ Ḥayyim 199:9.

63. R. Ḥayyim David Halevi, *Mayim Ḥayyim,* responsum 10, pp. 49f.

64. *Shulḥan Arukh,* Oraḥ Ḥayyim 186:1.

65. Berakhot 6:1, 45a.

66. *Tur Shulḥan Arukh,* Oraḥ Ḥayyim 199. R. Eliezer Berkovits argues that in our contemporary situation, "there is every justification" for accepting this opinion as a practical matter. Eliezer Berkovits, *Jewish Women in Time and Torah* (Hoboken, N.J.: Ktav, 1990), p. 92.

67. Ibid., Ḥiddushei Hagahot, n. 2

68. Baḥ, *Tur Shulḥan Arukh* 199, s.v. *ve-rabi yehudah ha-kohen.*

69. Taz, *Shulḥan Arukh,* Oraḥ Ḥayyim 199, n. 2.

70. *Shulḥan Arukh,* Oraḥ Ḥayyim 183:7.

71. Ibid. Rema's gloss. Cf. Baḥ to *Tur Shulḥan Arukh* 193, s.v. *u-mihu.*

72. Berakhot 45b.

73. Ibid., s.v. *im ratzu ein mezamnim.*

74. Perishah, *Tur Shulḥan Arukh* 199, n. 5.

75. *Shulḥan Arukh,* Oraḥ Ḥayyim 199:7.

76. Meiri, *Bet ha-Beḥirah,* Berakhot, chap. 7, third mishnah.

77. *Shulḥan Arukh,* Oraḥ Ḥayyim 197, 199:1.

78. Ibid. 552:8.

79. Ibid., *Magen Avraham,* n. 9.

80. *Mishnah Berurah* to *Shulḥan Arukh,* Oraḥ Ḥayyim 199, n. 12.

81. Berakhot 19b.

82. Ḥagigah 22a, Tosafot, s.v. *keman.*

83. Baḥ to *Tur Shulḥan Arukh 689,* s.v. *u-ba'al.*

At Our Life-Cycle Celebrations

84. Sharon Strassfeld and Michael Strassfeld, *The Second Jewish Catalog* (Philadelphia: Jewish Publication Society, 1976), pp. 31–37.

85. Sharon Strassfeld and Michael Strassfeld, "An Appropriate Ceremony for Daughters," *Sh'ma* 14/264, Dec. 23, 1983, pp. 27f.

86. Judith Bleich, "The Symbolism in Innovative Rituals," *Sh'ma* 14/264, Dec. 23, 1983, pp. 25ff.

87. R. Jonathan Sacks, "Creativity and Innovation in Halakhah," in *Rabbinic Authority and Personal Autonomy,* ed. Moshe Z. Sokol (Northvale: Jason Aronson, 1992), pp. 149–155.

88. Some of the texts traditionally recited by Sephardim on these occasions can be found in Aharon Cohen, *Zeved ha-Bat* (Jerusalem, 1990).

89. R. Moshe Sternbach, *Teshuvot ve-Hanagot* (Jerusalem, 5746 [1986]), responsum 195, p. 72; R. Ovadiah Yosef, *Yehave Da'at,* vol. 4, responsum 15, pp. 75–78.

90. This, R. Yosef observes, is the source some use to allow men and women to sit together and sing zemirot.

91. R. Ovadiah Yosef, *Yehave Da'at,* loc. cit.

92. R. Ovadiah Yosef, *Siddur Or va-Derekh le-bat Yisrael* (Jerusalem: Yeshivat Or va-Derekh, 1988).

93. R. Yehiel Yaakov Weinberg, *Seridei Esh,* vol. 3 (Jerusalem: Mosad Harav Kook, 1977), responsum 93, p. 297.

94. Ibid., p. 298.

95. R. Moshe Feinstein, *Iggerot Mosheh,* Oraḥ Ḥayyim, part 1 (New York: Moriah, 1959), responsum 104, p. 170. He argues that the synagogue may not be used for matters which are purely reshut (permitted but not obligatory), the category to which bat mitzvah celebrations should be assigned. Most synagogues today, however, are regularly used for activities that are permitted but not obligatory, such as lectures.

96. R. J. David Bleich, "Sabbath Candles for Young Girls," *Tradition* 16, no. 1 (Summer 1976): 150–155.

97. *Shulḥan Arukh,* Oraḥ Ḥayyim 271:2.

98. R. Ovadiah Yosef, *Yabbi'a Omer,* vol. 6 (Jerusalem: Porat Yosef, 1976), Oraḥ Ḥayyim, responsum 29, pp. 96–99.

99. One yeshiva elementary school educator conducted a group bat mitzvah celebration on a Sunday morning. The sixth-grade girls rehearsed all term for a musical cantata that include singing and dancing (but no *divrei Torah*); each girl received candlesticks. It would be interesting to see what a parallel boys' celebration would be.

100. R. Binyamin Adler, *Hilkhot ve-Halikhot Bar Mitzvah* (Jerusalem: Sefarim Or ha-Torah, 5734 [1974]), pp. 77–81.

101. R. Isaac Nissim, "Al birkhat barukh she-petarani," *No'am* 7 (5724 [1964]): 1–5; R. Ovadiah Yosef, *Yabbi'a Omer,* pt. 6, Oraḥ Ḥayyim, responsum 29, pp. 96–99.

102. R. Elyakim G. Elinson, *Ha-Ishah ve-ha-Mitzvot,* vol. 1 (Jerusalem: Jewish Agency, 5734 [1974]), pp. 181–184.

103. R. Sheraya Deblinsky, *Sova Semahot* (Jerusalem and New York: Feldheim, 5731 [1971]).

104. Ibid., p. 78, n. 70. In turn, of course, *Sova Sehmahot* becomes the cited source for the ruling in Aaron Felder, *Oholei Yeshurun,* vol. 1 (New York, 1980), p. 30, that "a woman may not recite any of the *Sheva Berochos.*"

105. In some sources, the term *birkhat ḥatanim* refers to all of the Sheva Berakhot (the blessing for wine plus the six specific blessings

in honor of the bride and groom); in others, only to the last and longest of them (Asher Bara).

106. At least with regard to the wedding feast, the *panim ḥadashot* must be "important" people. *Ḥiddushei ha-Ritva* (Ketubbot 7b) postulates that part of the definition of "important" is the ability to make up the quorum required for the recitation of the Sheva Berakhot. Thus he rules that a woman cannot qualify for *panim ḥadashot* even though she is otherwise important. On the other hand, *Ḥiddushei Ḥatam Sofer* (Ketubbot 7a, s.v. *be-makhelot*) allowed women to be *panim ḥadashot* (but R. Menasheh Klein, in *Mishneh Halakhot,* vol. 2, responsa 27–48, and vol. 7, responsum 246, felt that this was only a theoretical approval).

107. Berakhot 6a.

108. Maharsha to ibid., s.v. *over.*

109. Radbaz to ibid., s.v. *mitzvat aseh.*

110. Rambam, *Mishneh Torah,* Hilkhot Avel 14:1.

111. R. Shaul Yisraeli, "Be-inyan Birkhat Ḥatanim ve-Shituf Ishah ba-Hen," *Barkai,* no. 1 (Summer 5743 [1983]), pp. 163–166.

112. *Shulḥan Arukh,* Oraḥ Ḥayyim 271:2.

113. Ketubbot 17a.

114. Even ha-Ezer 65.

115. Massekhet Soferim 19:11.

116. Rambam, *Mishneh Torah,* Hilkhot Berakhot 2:1–11.

117. Berakhot 7b.

118. Kiddushin 41b.

119. A puzzling reference to this exclusionary phrase is found in Kesef Mishneh's commentary at the end of halakhah 10. Printed in brackets (and missing from the first printed edition), it says that "It seems to be obvious [that slaves and minors cannot say this blessing], as they may not join to make up the quorum of ten [adult free men] and *a fortiori* cannot say the blessing." This would, of course, also exclude women. But aside from the fact that it too ignores Rambam's deliberate change of language, he made this ruling in halakhah 9, which refers to an individual's additional blessing, which does not require the presence of a quorum.

Moreover, the *a fortiori* argument is invalid. There is no principle that individuals who do not qualify to establish a minyan are excluded from saying the prayers that depend on the existence of that minyan. The Mishnah which sets out the requirement of ten adult free men to say *birkhat ḥatanim* requires the same minyan for the public reading of the Torah and Haftarah. But minors today regularly read from the Torah and say the Haftarah, and women were originally allowed aliyot to the Torah. (Apparently the women also said Barekhu, the opening call for an aliyah, which requires a minyan. Ḥatam Sofer points out [*Ḥatam Sofer,* Oraḥ Ḥayyim (Pressburg, 1879), responsum 66] that, while originally only the first and last oleh recited *birkhat ha-Torah,* from the time of the institution of the aliyot for the Shabbat reading *each* oleh recited Barekhu even though the berakhot were not said.) Similarly, women and minors say the Mourner's Kaddish, which also requires the presence of a male minyan.

120. Even ha-Ezer 62:4–7.

121. Thus, for example, R. Shelomoh Kluger (*Ha-Elef Lekha Shelomoh,* Oraḥ Ḥayyim, responsum 93) rules that if three men (including the groom) ate at the meal, and seven other men who did not eat are present, Sheva Berakhot may be said (if *panim ḥadashot* and the bride and groom are present) even though there is no zimmun ba-shem. The minyan required for Sheva Berakhot is present, and the obligation for zimmun exists.

122. R. Moshe Feinstein, *Iggerot Mosheh,* Oraḥ Ḥayyim, part 1 (New York: Moriah, 5719 [1959]), responsum 56, pp. 129ff.

123. Quoted in R. David Auerbach, *Halikhot Beitah* (Jerusalem, 5743 [1983]), p. 94, n. 14.

124. R. David Auerbach to Joel B. Wolowelsky, 18 Ḥeshvan 5747 (November 20, 1987).

125. R. Ovadiah Yosef, *Yehave Da'at,* vol. 4, responsum 15, n. **, pp. 77f.

126. R. Moshe Halevi Steinberg, *Mesarvei Yam* (5752 [1992]), responsum 85, p. 96.

127. R. Aaron Soloveitchik, *Od Yisrael Yosef Beni Hai* (Yeshivas Brisk, 1993), no. 32, p. 100.

128. Rambam, Hilkhot Ishut 3:23.

129. Ibid. 3:17.

130. *Shulḥan Arukh,* Even ha-Ezer 34:1, Bet Shmuel, n. 1.

131. R. Azarya Berzon, "Birkhat ḥatanim," *Teḥumin* 6 (5745 [1985]): 101–117.

132. Eugene B. Borowitz, *Exploring Jewish Ethics* (Detroit: Wayne State University Press, 1990), p. 391.

133. R. Norman E. Frimer and Dov I. Frimer, "Reform Marriage in Contemporary Halakhic Responsa," *Tradition* 21, no. 3 (Fall 1984), p. 12.

In Our Synagogues

134. As a practical matter, when shuls are now built or remodeled, thought is often given to the question of how to construct as unisolating a meḥitzah as possible; one going right down the middle of the shul seems the most logical.

135. One of the arguments against women's prayer groups is that they deprive women of the opportunity to pray with a minyan.

136. The question of a woman being a cantor relates primarily to the fact that women have different obligations in regard to liturgical prayer. Thus, for example, in searching for a halakhic justification for a woman cantor, Joel Roth proposes a paradigm in which women would undertake an obligation that surpasses that of men. "On the Ordination of Women as Rabbis," in *The Ordination of Women as Rabbis: Studies and Responsa,* ed. Simon Greenberg (New York, 1988), pp. 127–187. In general, his proposal has not been well received. See Gidon Rothstein, "The Roth Responsum on the Ordination of Women," *Tradition* 24, no. 1 (Fall 1988): 104–11, and the exchange between Roth and Rothstein, "Communications," *Tradition* 24, no. 4 (Summer 1989), pp. 112–114. See also Judith Hauptman, "Women and Prayer: An Attempt to Dispel Some Fallacies," *Judaism* 42, no. 1 (Winter 1993), pp. 94–105, and Michael Broyde, Joel B. Wolowelsky, and Judith Hauptman, "Further on Women as Prayer Leaders and Their Role in Communal Prayer: An Exchange," *Judaism* 42, no. 4 (Fall 1993), pp. 387–393.

137. See Malbim, *Be'er ha-Millot* to Psalms 82:3.

138. R. Boruch Epsztejn [Barukh Epstein], *Makor Barukh* (Vilna: Romm, 1928), pt. 4, chap. 46, sec. 3, p. 981. The significance of this memoir is discussed in Don Seeman, "The Silence of Rayna

Batya: Torah, Suffering, and Rabbi Barukh Epstein's 'Wisdom of Women,'" *Torah u-Madda Journal* 6 (1995–96), pp. 91–128.

139. R. Barukh Epstein, *My Uncle the Netziv,* trans. Moshe Dombey (Jerusalem: ArtScroll/Mesorah, 1988).

140. R. Moshe Halevi Spero, "The Didactic-Psychological Function of Three Rabbinic Blessings," *Proceedings of the Association of Orthodox Jewish Scientists* 8 (1987), p. 114.

141. R. Emanuel Feldman, "An Articulate *Berakha,*" *Tradition* 29, no. 4 (Summer 1995), p. 73.

142. David Shatz, "Practical Endeavor and the Torah u-Madda Debate," *Torah u-Madda Journal* 3 (1991–92), pp. 101.

143. R. Feldman, "Articulate *Berakha,*" p. 71.

144. *Maggid Mishneh,* Hilkhot Ḥametz u-Matzah 5:20.

145. To cite one example, a recent brochure announcing a conference sponsored by Agudah on the interface of the professions and halakhah read like a program for an old Yavneh convention; the cover picture of the clean-shaven young man with a kippah could have been provided by Yeshiva University Public Relations.

146. R. Aharon Worms, *Me'orei Or,* vol. 4 (= *Be'er Sheva*) (Metz, 1831), p. 20.

147. R. Naftali Zvi Roth, "Azkarah ve-haftarah ve-kaddish yatom," *Talpioth* 7, nos. 2–4 (Tishrei 5721 [1961]), pp. 369–381.

148. R. Joseph B. Soloveitchik, "A Eulogy for the Talner Rebbe," in *Shiurei Harav: A Conspectus of Public Lectures of Rabbi Joseph B. Soloveitchik,* ed. Joseph Epstein (Hoboken, N.J.: Ktav, 1994), p. 70.

149. R. Roth, "Azkarah ve-haftarah ve-kaddish yatom," p. 375.

150. R. Ya'ir Ḥayyim Bacharach, *Ḥavvot Ya'ir,* responsum 22.

151. R. Yehudah Ashkenazi, *Be'er Heitev,* commentary to Oraḥ Ḥayyim, sec. 132, n. 5, p. 27, in vol. 2 of standard *Mishnah Berurah.*

152. R. Ḥayyim Mordecai Margoliyot, *Sha'arei Teshuvah,* n. 5, in *Mishnah Berurah* ad loc.

153. There is nothing surprising about allowing a female mourner to say Kaddish unaccompanied by anyone else. The private minyanim which many *posekim* allowed to be set up for female mourners were by definition services where the mourner alone said Kaddish.

Any objections concerning *kol ishah, tzeniut* (modesty), etc., would apply equally to both private and synagogue minyanim, as they would to a woman's saying *birkhat ha-gomel.*

154. The core of the members of this famous shul is made up of former students of the Mirrer Yeshiva who came to the United States after World War II by way of Shanghai.

155. I am grateful to Dr. Eliach for sharing this material from her forthcoming book, *The Shtetl,* soon to be published by Little, Brown. Dr. Eliach's photo collection of the townspeople of Eisheshok is part of the permanent exhibition at the National Holocaust Museum in Washington, D.C.

156. This practice found its way to America. Writing about an Orthodox synagogue in New Bedford, Massachusetts, in the early twentieth century, Herman Eliot Snyder says: "Despite this strict separation of the men and women, a young girl, perhaps sixteen years old, would enter the men's section to recite the Kaddish for a parent. No one ever made protest or even a comment." Snyder, "The American Synagogue World of Yesterday, 1901–1925," *American Jewish Archives* 42, no. 1 (Spring–Summer 1990), p. 72.

157. R. Moshe Feinstein, *Iggerot Mosheh,* Oraḥ Ḥayyim, part 5 (Jerusalem: Ḥemed, 5756 [1996]), responsum 12, p. 20.

158. R. Yosef Eliyahu Henkin, *Sefer Teshuvot Ibra,* vol. 2 (New York: Ezrat Torah, 1989), "Amirat kaddish al yedi ha-bat," no. 4, pp. 3–5. This is a reprint of his article by the same name that appeared in *Hapardes* 38, no. 6, pp. 5–6. R. Henkin's student and grandson, R. Yehudah Herzl Henkin, published an extensive discussion and explanation of that decision in his "Amirat kaddish al yedei ishah ve-tziruf la-minyan me-ezrat nashim," *Hadarom,* no. 54 (Sivan 5745 [1985]): 34–48, reprinted in his *Benei Banim,* vol. 2 (1992), responsum 6, pp. 23–30.

159. R. Aaron Felder, *Yesodei Smochos,* part 1 (New York: Balsham, 1974), sec. 4.1, p. 50. Emphasis added.

160. Ibid., p. 123, n. 1.

161. R. Yekutiel Greenwald, *Kol Bol al Avelut,* vol. 1 (New York: Feldheim, 1965), p. 375. *Kol Bo*'s suggestion is not necessarily a practical one. As we have noted, when a woman comes to shul on a weekday to answer amen to the men's Kaddish, she usually finds that the daily morning minyan has no meḥitzah.

162. R. Shlomo Halevi Wahrman, *She'erit Yosef,* vol. 2 (New York: Balsham, 1981), pp. 299f.

163. R. Yisrael Meir Lau, *Yahel Yisrael* (Jerusalem, 5752 [1992]), vol. 2, responsum 90, p. 479.

164. While this approach is unpalatable, the opposing position of searching for every possible ḥeter instead of every possible ḥumrah is likewise intellectually dishonest and unacceptable.

165. R. Aaron Soloveitchik, *Od Yisrael Yosef Beni Hai,* no. 32, p. 100.

166. R. Menasheh Klein, *Mishneh Halakhot,* vol. 1, *Tinyana* (5752 [1992]), responsum 650, p. 467.

167. *Shulḥan Arukh,* Oraḥ Ḥayyim 669:1.

168. R. Yitzhak Yosef, *Yalkut Yosef* (a compendium of the decisions of R. Ovadiah Yosef), vol. 5 (Mo'adim), Dinei Keriat ha-Megillah, par. 12, n. 21, pp. 288f. He explicitly notes that *kol ishah* is not a consideration in this matter.

169. R. Tzvi Pesaḥ Frank, *Mirae'ei Kodesh: Ḥanukkah/Purim* (Jerusalem: Makhon ha-Rav Frank, 5752 [1982]), no. 29, pp. 131–132.

170. *Mishnah Berurah* 669:4, n. 7.

171. Sh'ar Tziyun, ibid., n. 15.

172. Quoted in R. Auerbach, *Halikhot Beitah,* p. 71.

173. R. Alfred S. Cohen, "Women and the Reading of the Megilla," *Journal of Halacha and Contemporary Society,* no. xxx. (Fall 1995), p. 37, n. 43.

174. *Shulḥan Arukh,* Oraḥ Ḥayyim 690:18.

175. Ran to Rif, Megillah 19b, s.v. *ha-kol kesherim.*

176. *Mikra'ei Kodesh,* no. 35, pp. 143ff.

177. *Shulḥan Arukh,* Oraḥ Ḥayyim 692:7; *Mishnah Berurah,* n. 8.

178. Ibid. 688:7, *Mishnah Berurah,* n. 20.

179. R. Eliezer Yehudah Waldenberg, *Tzitz Eliezer,* vol. 13 (Jerusalem, 5745 [1985]), responsum 73, p. 145.

180. As with a zimmun, a group of either men or women alone may form the quorum, but a coed group may not.

181. R. Ovadiah Yosef, *Yabbi'a Omer,* vol. 8 (Jerusalem, 5755 [1995]), Oraḥ Ḥayyim, responsum 56, p. 246.

182. R. Abba Bronspigl, "Minyanim meyuḥadim le-nashim," *Hadarom,* no. 54 (Sivan 5745 [1985]), pp. 51–53; R. Hershel Schacter,

"Be-inyanei beit kenesset," *Or ha-Mizrach,* Tishrei 5746 (1985), pp. 328–332; idem, "Ze-i lakh be-ikvei ha-tzon," *Beit Yitzhak,* 5745 (1985), pp. 118–134.

183. R. Avraham Weiss, *Women at Prayer: A Halakhic Analysis of Women's Prayer Groups* (Hoboken, N.J.: Ktav, 1990).

184. Ibid., p. 98.

185. Ibid., p. 108.

186. Ibid., p. 82, n. 40.

187. See the moving anecdote "The Grip of the Holy Letters" in Yaffa Eliach, *Hasidic Tales of the Holocaust* (New York: Oxford University Press, 1982), pp. 202–204.

188. Robert Harris, "The First Two Aliyot for a Bat Kohen and a Bat Levi," *Responsa of the Va'ad Halacha of the Rabbinical Assembly of Israel* (Jerusalem, 1989), vol. 3, p. viii (Hebrew sec., pp. 31–33).

189. R. Moshe Sofer, *Ḥatam Sofer,* Oraḥ Ḥayyim (Pressburg, 1879), responsum 66.

190. Berakhot 45a.

191. R. Berman, "The Status of Women in Halakhic Judaism," *Tradition* 14, no. 2 (Fall 973): 21f.

In Our Schools

192. David Berger, "A Symposium on Divided and Distinguished Worlds," *Tradition* 26, no. 2 (Winter 1992), p. 10.

193. R. Yoel Teitelbaum, "Ma-amar lashon ha-kodesh," *Va-Yoel Moshe* (Brooklyn, N.Y.: Jerusalem Publishers, 5721 [1961]), secs. 30–50, pp. 436–453.

194. R. Joseph B. Soloveitchik, "Redemption, Prayer, Talmud Torah," *Tradition* 17, no. 2 (Spring 1978), p. 69.

195. R. Israel Meir Hakohen (Kagan), *Likkutei Halakhot,* Sotah 20b.

196. In June 1991, Rabbi Jeffrey R. Woolf, executive chairman of the Orthodox Roundtable, wrote to an official of a New York-area yeshiva that when the Rav established the Maimonides Yeshiva, he "explicitly provided for co-education in grades K–12, thus ensuring equal education for all enrolled in the school. Perhaps even more significant is the fact that until the time of his illness and subsequent retirement, he never veered from the position that such an

arrangement was legitimate and Halakhically justified, ab initio, and not a begrudged ex post facto concession. Indeed the current administration of the school, under the guidance of the Rav's daughter, Dr. Atarah Twersky, bears this fact out fully. (I am going out of my way to emphasize this point, as there is a significant amount of conscious 'historical revisionism' in the Orthodox community which seeks to portray Rav Soloveitchik's position in a different light." The letter received wide though informal circulation in the ḥinnukh community. See also Rabbi Beni Brama, "Kavim le-Shitato Rambam," in Amnon Shapira, *Ḥevra Meurevet* (Tel Aviv: Bnei Akiva Youth Organization, 1982), pp. 6–7.

197. *Mekor Barukh,* pp. 123f.

198. R. Aharon Lichtenstein, "Torah Study for Women," *Ten Da'at* 3, no. 3 (Spring 1989), p. 8. Translated by R. Jack Bieler from "Fundamental Problems Regarding the Education of Women," in *Ha-Ishah ve-Ḥinnukha,* ed. Ben-Zion Rosenfeld (Kfar Saba: Emunah, 1980).

199. Devora Steinmetz, "A Dream Deferred," *Darshan,* no. 3 (Spring 1996), p. 4.

200. R. Lichtenstein, "Torah Study for Women," p. 7.

201. R. Menaḥem M. Schneersohn, "Ḥovat ha-nashim be-limmud ha-Torah u-ve-ḥinnukh," delivered Lag baOmer, April 13, 1990; printed in *Kefar Habad News-letter,* 26 Iyyar 5750 (April 21, 1990), pp. 5–7.

202. David I. Bernstein, "Symposium on Women and Jewish Education," *Tradition* 28, no. 3 (Spring 1994), p. 11.

203. R. Lichtenstein, "Torah Study for Women," p. 8.

204. Indeed, it is hard to imagine, say, Nehama Leibowitz garnering more respect by virtue of some rabbinic ordination.

205. R. Eliyahu Bakshi-Doron, *Binyan Av* (Jerusalem, 1982), responsum 65, p. 287. See also *Encyclopedia Talmudit,* vol. 8, s.v., *hora'ah,* p. 494, and the sources brought there in n. 109.

206. Chana Henkin, "Symposium on Women and Jewish Education," *Tradition* 28, no. 3 (Spring 1994), p. 33.

207. Some feminists maintain that men and women see the world differently, and that women would naturally have created a system of secular jurisprudence that differed in substance and direction

from that created by men. Similar criticisms have been raised against halakhah, charging that Jewish law would have a very different character if women had been the major halakhists. It is therefore worthwhile to take note of Steven F. Fridell's study showing that, even though women have had little day-to-day input in the development of Jewish law, halakhah incorporates the major components of what would be "feminine jurisprudence." Fridell, "The 'Different Voice' in Jewish Law: Some Parallels to a Feminist Jurisprudence," *Indiana Law Journal* 67 (1992), p. 915–949.

208. Perhaps for this reason, very few Modern Orthodox men are vying for jobs as pulpit rabbis.

Conclusion

209. Joseph C. Kaplan, "A Women's Sefer Torah," *Sh'ma* 14, 274 (May 11, 1984), p. 11f.

210. Berger, "Symposium on Women and Jewish Education," p. 10.